FAVOUR OF GOD

A practical guide to always experience the Favour of God

BY

Dr. Bobby Y.K. Sung

www.sungministry.com

Published in United Kingdom
by Agape Behaviour publishing

For more information contact

Telephone: +44 (0) 8432 894 017
Mobile: +44 (0) 7939 996 111
www.agapebehaviourpublishing.com
info@agapebehaviourpublishing.com
www.sungministry.com
Print ISBN: 978-0-9550575-8-8
EBook ISBN: 978-0-9550575-9-5

Contents

Introduction: Favour of God

There are many things in this world that we do not understand. We sometimes see people who have done bad things succeed in life and often those who do good things appear to be less successful. We wonder to ourselves "what is going on?" We may try to use our own judgement to assess what is happening in other people's lives, without fully understanding their situation. Only God knows all things, He is the almighty and He is the all knowing God.

I have met some people who seem to be successful at everything, no matter what they do. If you put them in business they are successful. If you put them in charge of Sunday school, they do a good job and they succeed. If you put them in a church steward team they also function well. These individuals appear to have miracle hands; they just prosper and excel in everything they do. Wherever they go and whatever they do, the favour of God is clearly evident within their life. God's presence is always with them.

In contrast some people are the complete opposite. Whatever they do has little or no success at all. If they go to the bank, they have to wait for a long time in the queue to be served. When their turn finally comes the bank counter staff say "sorry, it's lunch time, we have to close this counter, the counter is closed."

When travelling by train, they arrive on time, but the door of the train closes one second early causing them to miss the train. Taking a bus to work, the bus stops several times to change driver. They go to park their car, they try to reverse the car for parking, take it easy, slowly. Slowly, they are reversing to park the car, but suddenly, a car comes from nowhere and parks in the space where they intended to park. Success just seems out of their reach. I have observed people like this in real life situations and it can be very disheartening. They go to numerous job interviews, always thinking they will get the job, but at the last minute the company chooses another candidate. Are any of these experiences familiar to you?

There was someone I knew whose life was a tragedy. He got married and brought his wife over from Hong Kong to Holland. Then his wife followed another person and divorced him. He got married again, then also divorced. He started again, a third time, but after some time, the third marriage also failed and he divorced again. Then, some years later, his son died in an accident. He himself also died from an accident when he was in his old age. It seemed that everything went wrong for him. No matter how hard he worked, no matter how good a person he was, it brought no success. It only brought tragedy after tragedy. Despite being a good hardworking person he endured a lot of heartache. It seems the favour of God was not in his life.

Although we do not know why some people live a painful life full of setbacks and others race through successfully with ease. One thing we are absolutely sure of is that God is love and God is good. He loves each one of us. God is just; He is faithful, powerful and all knowing.

In this book, we will try to explore the subject of the favour of God and how we can receive the favour of God in our lives.

Appreciation

Thanks be to God, my heavenly Father. It is He who gave me the wisdom to write this book, all the resources I have are from Him.

Thank you so much to my daughter Oi Yin and Pastor Eliran Wong for your excellent work and spending many hours to work hard on this book with me. God bless you.

Special thanks to my friend Dr. Mohammed T.S. Johnson, teacher at The Excel University www.theexceluniversity.org & senior Pastor at Excel Centre Church, UK. He encouraged me to write the book, and helped me from start to finish on this project.

God bless you.

About The Author

Pastor Bobby is the founder and Senior Pastor of Emmanuel Chinese Church, London. He first encountered the Lord in Christmas 1986 after a friend shared the gospel with him. After receiving and accepting Jesus as his personal Lord and Saviour, he was filled with an earnest desire to share his newly found faith with everyone he met.

His zeal and passion for the Lord inspired his family to know and follow Jesus Christ. Shortly after his conversion, it became apparent that the Holy Spirit had baptised him in a unique and extraordinary manner. After being filled with the Spirit, Pastor Bobby found himself naturally evangelising and ministering in a variety of supernatural spiritual gifts.

Since the day of his salvation, the fire of God has burned incessantly in his heart. This is reflected in the rapid growth of his ministry as his passion for Jesus continues to ignite, inspire and touch the lives of many.

In January 1999, he gave up his business in response to God's calling for him to serve in full-time ministry. His greatest passions are reaching out to the lost, nurturing new believers and training passionate leaders of the Kingdom. Pastor Bobby has three grown-up children. His wife serves the Lord alongside him as a great and powerful intercessor in the church.

This book will encourage readers to seek and experience the favour of God in their lives.

For more titles from this author see:

www.sungministry.com

Foreword

Pastor Bobby Sung is the Pastor of Emmanuel Chinese Church in the heart of China Town, London UK. He is passionate to preach the gospel of the kingdom. His ministry is always filled with God's grace and power. He lifts up the name of Jesus Christ all the time, demonstrating the power of God with healing and miracles. God empowers His words through him to bring transformation to many.

There are many questions that people have asked when it comes to the subject of 'Grace'. Pastor Bobby skilfully takes you on a journey explaining what Grace is and what one may have to encounter when fulfilling the purpose that God has for their life.

In this book, he skilfully tackles the subject of Grace and the life that we as Children of God must live in order to obtain God's Favour over our lives. The words penned in this book are a reminder to the reader that one must position themselves with the right mind to speak words of faith to obtain God's Favour in your life.

I pray that as you read through each page, you are blessed, encouraged, edified and your lives are enriched in the fullness that all God has in store for you.

'But to each one of us grace was given according to the measure of Christ's gift'. Ephesians 4 v 7.

BISHOP JOHN FRANCIS
RUACH CITY CHURCH LONDON, UK &
PHILADELPHIA, USA

Rev. Dr Bobby Sung is a man of God that loves people. I believe his genuine passion for God and the lost naturally triggers the favour of God in his life. I also believe that when you have the FAVOUR of God flowing in your life you can truly experience the luxury of Jesus highlighted in the Holy Bible **John 10 verse** *10. My prayer is that all who read this practical guide will truly experience the incredible favour of God.* **Dr. Mohammed T.S Johnson, Excel Life Church www.theexceluniversity.org**

Chapter 1
What is the Favour of God?

The English word ‘favour’, appears in the Bible, is translated from the Old Testament Hebrew word, חֵן (Genesis 18:3). The New Testament Greek word, χάρις (Luke 1:30). The same Hebrew and Greek word are also translated as grace (Psalm 45:2; Luke 2:40). Therefore, “favour” and “grace” are inseparable and sometimes are used interchangeable, as they are the only different translations of the same original words.

Objectively, the original language meaning to cause favourable regard. Gracefulness, grace, loveliness of form, graciousness of speech. Subjectively, it means grace, graciousness, kindness, goodwill, favour; a sense of favour received, thanks and gratitude.

THE FAVOUR OF GOD IS:

God is the source of our favour.

For the Lord God is a sun and shield; the Lord bestows favor and honor; no good thing does he withhold from those whose walk is blameless. **(Psalm 84:11)**

When God gives you favour it means He likes you and is pleased with you. In the context of this book we consider favour to be a special privilege or advantage, granted by God. God treats differently those whom He favours.

Favour of God is a blessing from God that you don't deserve but He just gives it to you. It is not based on your own effort, your own merit or on your good character or good deeds.

You may say "today it is not my day, I have no luck and nothing good can happen to me," or you may say "it is ordained in my life already, no matter what I do, the heavens have already set up everything for me." These people believe God has already set some things up for them, when they step into it, then it is their luck.

You may think the favour of God is a coincidence that just happens. No. It is not coincidence as I said before; it is not luck either. We will explain more on this topic in our next chapter about chosen and election.

The favour of God can be displayed or manifested in many different forms, in many areas of our lives. Your business, family, career, health, marriage, ministry and church.

People receive the favour of God because of His kindness, his love and his mercy towards us.

The favour of God is from God alone. From His throne of grace He pours out His blessings, His grace and His love into our lives.

For surely, O LORD, you bless the righteous; you surround them with your favour as with shield. **(Psalm 5:12)**

ONE TOUCH OF GOD'S FAVOUR CAN CHANGE YOUR DESTINY.

God can do for you in a second, that which could take years to accomplish alone. One touch of God can change your destiny, can change your business, or change your whole life, just one touch.

Sometimes we work very hard and see no result at all. We use a lot of effort and energy, diligently wearing ourselves out. But somehow despite all the sweat and tears it seems we are going nowhere.

When God's favour comes into our life, it changes everything, our situations become transformed.

GOD'S FAVOUR IS READY FOR YOU, HE SURROUND YOU WITH FAVOUR.

Chapter 2
You are chosen for God's Favour

What good is it if we know about God's favour but it seems to have nothing to do with our lives? Thanks be to our God! The Bible doesn't just tell us about God's favour, but it actually proclaims that we are chosen for God's favour.

ELECTION AND FAVOUR

In the Bible, election and favour are always inseparable. Let me give you some examples below:

- Adam

God blessed them and said to them, "Be fruitful and increase in number; fill the earth and subdue it. Rule over the fish in the sea and the birds in the sky and over every living creature that moves on the ground." ***(Genesis 1:28)***

God chose Adam to be the first human being, God blessed him (favour) and made a covenant with him. God has a purpose in his life. **(Genesis 1:26-27; Malachi 2:15; Hosea 6:7**)

- Abel

Now Abel kept flocks, and Cain worked the soil. In the course of time Cain brought some of the fruits of the soil as an offering to the Lord. And Abel also brought an offering—fat portions from some of the firstborn of his flock. The Lord looked with favor on Abel and his offering, but on Cain and his offering he did not look with favor. So Cain was very angry, and his face was downcast. ***(Genesis 4:2-5)***

Abel's heart was right before God. He obeyed God and did what He asked him to do, as in the book of Hebrew 11:4 By faith Abel offered God a better sacrifice than Cain did.

- Noah

But Noah found favour in the eyes of the LORD. ***(Genesis 6:8)***

His whole family were saved in the flood and escape God's judgement.

- Abraham

Abraham received the favour of God.

The Lord had said to Abram, "Go from your country, your people and your father's household to the land I will show you." I will make you into a great nation, and I will bless you; I will make your name great, and you will be a blessing. I will bless those who bless you, and whoever curses you I will curse; and all peoples on earth will be blessed through you." **(Genesis 12:1-3)**

God chose Abraham among all the people, to bless and favour him.

- Isaac

Then God said, "Yes, but your wife Sarah will bear you a son, and you will call him Isaac. I will establish my covenant with him as an everlasting covenant for his descendants after him. **(Genesis 17:19)**

But my covenant I will establish with Isaac, whom Sarah will bear to you by this time next year." **(Genesis 17:21)**

God favoured Isaac and chose him over Ishmael.

- Jacob

Not only that, but Rebekah's children were conceived at the same time by our father Isaac. Yet, before the twins were born or had done anything good or bad—in order that God's purpose in election might stand: not by works but by him who calls—she was told, "The older will serve the younger." Just as it is written: "Jacob I loved, but Esau I hated." What then shall we say? Is God unjust? Not at all! For he says to Moses, "I will have mercy on whom I have mercy, and I will have compassion on whom I have compassion." ***(Romans 9:10-15)***

Jacob was chosen even before his mother Rebekah gave birth to him. God chose Jacob and favoured him even before he had even done anything. God's election and favour is only a matter of God's sovereign choice, it is given by grace. In ancient societies, it was customary for the firstborn son to receive favour in the sight of his parents and siblings. Even though Jacobs' elder twin brother Esau was conscious of the favour his younger brother received. The Lord blessed Jacob throughout his whole life. He was so desperate for God's favour that he once struggled with an angel in order to get the blessings.

Then the man said, "Let me go, for it is daybreak."

But Jacob replied, "I will not let you go unless you bless me." ***(Genesis 32:26)***

- Joseph

When his master saw that the Lord was with him and that the Lord gave him success in everything he did, 4 Joseph found favor in his eyes and became his attendant. Potiphar put him in charge of his household, and he entrusted to his care everything he owned. ***(Genesis 39: 3-4)***

Joseph was successful in everything he did. He was promoted in Egypt to be the second in command to Pharaoh. Joseph received the favour of God

- Ruth

Ruth was a poor Moabite widow, who appeared to have everything going against her. Ruth's husband died young and she was in a foreign land. Despite this she believed God and received the favour of God in her life. She became the great grandmother of King David.

"May I continue to find favour in your eyes, my Lord." **(Ruth 2:13)**

- David

After removing Saul, he made David their king. God testified concerning him: 'I have found David son of Jesse, a man after my own heart; he will do everything I want him to do.' **(Acts 13:22)**

When we study David's life, it is evident that he understands the favour of God. The book of Psalms was written by David, Psalm 23 it was so beautifully written.

You prepare a table before me in the presence of my enemies. You anoint my head with oil;

my cup overflows. Surely your goodness and love will follow me all the days of my life, and I will dwell in the house of the Lord forever. **(Psalm 23:5-6)**

- Solomon

Solomon received the favour of God. He built the temple for God and he was given incomparable wisdom.

God gave Solomon wisdom and very great insight, and a breadth of understanding as measureless as the sand on the seashore. Solomon's wisdom was greater than the wisdom of all the people of the East, and greater than all the wisdom of Egypt. He was wiser than anyone else, including Ethan the Ezrahite—wiser than Heman, Kalkol and Darda, the sons of Mahol. And his fame spread to all the surrounding nations. **(1 Kings 4:29-31)**

The Bible has plenty of examples, but I have given only a few, to illustrate that God selects His people and shows them favour.

Some of us may think that God chooses some people over others, and the election is totally out of God's sovereignty. People may feel hopeless because they are not sure if they are chosen. They may wrongly equate God's sovereignty as random choice. They think some people are chosen out of luck, but some people are not. The Bible, however, assures all of us that we are all chosen in Jesus.

YOU ARE CHOSEN THROUGH JESUS

God's elections or choices are all sovereign but not random, not without purpose. One point I would like to highlight is that all of the elected individuals I have just mentioned were related to Jesus. All Old Testament elections were because of the election of Jesus. Every person related to Jesus will be blessed and favoured.

To put it this way, they were chosen because of Jesus.

The Bible says as follows; *The law is only a shadow of the good things that are coming—not the realities themselves. For this reason it can never, by the same sacrifices repeated endlessly year after year, make perfect those who draw near to worship.* **(Hebrews 10:1)**

Adam was created and chosen because God was seeking a 'godly offspring (Malachi 2:15).' Even after the fall, God still favoured people and promised that Eve would give birth to 'an offspring,' who 'will strike the head' of the devil (Genesis 3:15-16). Afterwards, the Bible keeps referring to this 'seed' as we see in Genesis 17:19.

Galatians 3:16 finally revealed to us that this very 'seed' is Jesus. No wonder through Adam and Eve and the whole family line down to Jesus, all people who are chosen, like Noah, Abraham, Isaac, Jacob, Judah even Ruth and many others, only because of Jesus.

We can see this truth especially in the case of Isaac and Jacob. Isaac was not the firstborn to Abraham and Jacob was not the firstborn to Isaac. However they were chosen because Jesus would be their descendant. (Romans 9:6-13) confirms this special election as well.

So as Judah who is the fourth son of Jacob, he is chosen because Jesus was ultimately born through the line of Judah. This is not a coincidence for God foretold this through the blessing of Jacob (Genesis 49:8-12).

Abel was chosen because the offering of the lamb foreshadowed the death of Jesus. Joseph and Moses were chosen because their lives foreshadowed Jesus. In one sentence, everything is about Jesus.

Because Jesus died for us, the whole world can have an opportunity to access the blessings of God. Every person, every living thing and event that relate to Him are blessed and favoured.

What about us? The good news is that we are all chosen because of Jesus. If God's election were random, many would run out of luck; *For God so loved the world that he gave his one and only*

Son, that whoever believes in him shall not perish but have eternal life. **(John 3:16)**

He makes sure the whole world can receive his salvation, grace and favour, by electing Jesus Christ. As the Bible says, now is the time of favour and salvation.

For he says, "In the time of my favor I heard you, and in the day of salvation I helped you." I tell you, now is the time of God's favor, now is the day of salvation. **(2 Corinthians 6:2)**

He was chosen before the creation of the world, but was revealed in these last times for your sake. **(1 Peter 1:20)**

For he chose us in him before the creation of the world to be holy and blameless in his sight.

In love he predestined us for adoption to sonship through Jesus Christ, in accordance with his pleasure and will— to the praise of his glorious grace, which he has freely given us in the One he loves. In him we have redemption through his blood, the forgiveness of sins, in accordance with the riches of God's grace that he lavished on us. With all wisdom and understanding, **(Ephesians 1:4-8)**

Our elections are all based on the election of Jesus Christ. Because Jesus is chosen, we are chosen in Him. Jesus was favoured in order for us to receive favour. Through the death of Jesus, we have the access to the throne of grace, i.e. The throne of favour.

Let us then approach God's throne of grace with confidence, so that we may receive mercy and find grace to help us in our time of need. **(Hebrews 4:16)**

Yes, God's favour is indeed available and ready for all of us. Therefore the next part of this book is very important. We will see how the favour of God works in people's lives and how we can engage in God's favour and activate God's favour in our lives.

Chapter 3
God's Favour makes you successful

Favour makes you successful. Below are some examples, and I will talk more on Joseph.

Nehemiah

Nehemiah knew that in order to be successful, he needed the favour of God.

Lord, let your ear be attentive to the prayer of this your servant and to the prayer of your servants who delight in revering your name. Give your servant success today by granting him favor in the presence of this man." ***(Nehemiah 1:11)***

Moses

Moses understood that the favour of God was very important. His success and failure depended solely on the favour of God.

Moses said to the Lord, "You have been telling me, 'Lead these people,' but you have not let me know whom you will send with me. You have said, 'I know you by name and you have found favor with me.' If you are pleased with me, teach me your ways so I may know you and continue to find favor with you. Remember that this nation is your people."

The Lord replied, "My Presence will go with you, and I will give you rest." Then Moses said to him, "If your Presence does not go with us, do not send us up from here. **(Exodus 33:12-15)**

Moses knew that success was only when God was with them.

Joseph

The Lord was with Joseph so that he prospered, and he lived in the house of his Egyptian master. When his master saw that the Lord was with him and that the Lord gave him success in everything he did, Joseph found favor in his eyes and became his attendant. Potiphar put him in charge of his household, and he entrusted to his care everything he owned. From the time he put him in charge of his household and of all that he owned, the Lord blessed the household of the Egyptian because of Joseph. The blessing of the Lord was on everything

Potiphar had, both in the house and in the field. ***(Genesis 39:2-5)***

SUCCESSFUL IN EVERYTHING

The Lord gave Joseph success in everything he did, something very obvious, he was successful in everything. The Lord was with Joseph and he prosper. Four times the text states that the Lord was with him. (Genesis 39:2,3,21,23)

When a person has the favour of God, that means God is walking with them and His presence is with them.

Success comes only when God is in the midst of what they are doing, Only when His presence is there.

Wouldn't it be awesome to have a generation of Josephs' in our church? Wouldn't you love Joseph to invest money on your behalf? You'd be sure to see a profitable return and a great blessing. Still we must be careful to remember that the blessing comes through Joseph from God.

If you put Joseph in charge of your business, he would certainly cause it to prosper. If you put him in charge of your country, he'll be the best

President. If you put him in charge of your ministry he would definitely make a great difference.

What was the secret of Joseph's success? Not a first class sales and marketing degree. Nor was it good strategy planning, it was quite simply the favour of God. Thus the Lord was with him. The Lord's favour was upon his life, because the LORD was with him. The LORD had a good plan for his life.

Joseph's life had a sad beginning, as his mother died when she gave birth to his younger brother Benjamin ***(Genesis 35:16-20).***

His father also favoured Rachel. He loved Rachel more than Leah, (Genesis 29:30) and he also favoured Joseph. He loved Joseph more than his other sons. **(Genesis 37:3)** His father had favourites.

Because of his father's favouritism, his brothers disliked him, they envied him (Genesis 37:11) ,they hated him (Genesis 37:4, 5, 8) Among Josephs' brothers were murderous and immoral men (Genesis 34:1, Genesis 35:22). He lived in a family full of favouritism, jealousy, bitterness, hatred and blame.

But in spite of all these negative circumstances, God favoured Joseph. Even though he had a sad beginning, a bad childhood and living in a family full of envy and hate, he still found success in everything he did. God's favour made his life different to others and he became successful in everything.

It is all about God's favour. God is no respecter of persons. He does not care about your background, whether you are poor or rich. God does not care which university you graduated from, God does not look at the things that man looks at. Man looks at the outward appearance, but the Lord looks at the heart. God looks at your heart.

Let us look at Joseph's life a little more. His life was quite turbulent and full of ups and downs. When he received a dreams from the Lord, he felt so excited and it was his high point in life. He eagerly shared the dreams with his brothers and it made the relationship worse.

His brothers were envious of him and hated him so much, as a result he was sold to Midianites and the Midianites then sold him in Egypt to Potiphar as a slave.

Nevertheless he was a success even in the lowest points of his life, because he trusted God.

The next phase in Joseph's life continued with ups and downs. His masters' wife tempted him to sleep with her. Because Joseph was handsome and was well built, she tempted him day by day. Not just once but day after day. Joseph refused to go to bed with her, he fled from the temptation, and that made his master's wife angry. He demonstrated his spiritual strength because he did not give into the temptation put before him.

Despite his master's wife lied and accused him of a crime he had not committed. She claimed he was guilty of rape, and Joseph was placed in prison as a result. But God was still with Joseph during this part of his life. Even in prison God showed himself to Joseph through his presence. Despite Joseph being at the lowest point of his life, he did not blame God. Even though Joseph did not understand what was going on in his life.

When his master heard the story his wife told him, saying, "This is how your slave treated me," he burned with anger. Joseph's master took him and put him in prison, the place where the king's prisoners were confined. But while Joseph was there in the prison, the Lord was with him; he showed him kindness and granted him favor in the eyes of the prison warden. So the warden put Joseph in charge of all those held in the prison, and he was made responsible for all that was done there. The warden paid no attention to anything under Joseph's care, because the Lord was with Joseph and gave him success in whatever he did. ***(Genesis 39:19-23)***

Even in prison God demonstrated His favour to Joseph, by allowing the warden to place him in charge of the prisoners. God does use bad situations to accomplish His good plan.

Some time later, the cupbearer and the baker of the king of Egypt offended their master, the king of Egypt. Pharaoh was angry with his two officials, the chief cupbearer and the chief baker, and put them in custody in the house of the captain of the guard, in the same prison where Joseph was confined. The captain of the guard assigned them to Joseph, and he attended them. After they had been in custody for some time, each of the two men—the cupbearer and the baker of the king of Egypt, who were being held in prison—had a dream the same night, and each dream had a meaning of its own. ***(Genesis 40:1-5)***

One day, two of Pharaoh's servants had a dream. He saw their faces were so sad and he began to talk with them. They said they each had a dream, but no one to interpret the dreams for them. So, Joseph interpreted the dreams for them, and both of the dreams came true.

He asked the cupbearer to remember him and show kindness to him, mention him to Pharaoh and get him out of the prison. True to Josephs' words the cupbearer was restored to his position and once again served the king, but forgot to mention Joseph and this became another setback as it caused Joseph to be in prison longer.

Two years later, Pharaoh had a dream. This time the chief cupbearer did remember Joseph and mentioned him to Pharaoh. Pharaoh sent for Joseph and he interpreted the dream. It was at this time that Joseph was promoted by Pharaoh to be in charge of the whole land of Egypt.

Joseph experiences good and bad times in his life, yet the Bible says he was a success in everything. Even when he was at the lowest point, sold to Egypt as a slave, falsely accused and put in prison, he was successful. Therefore, success is not only the outcome of what we do. So often, when people experience bad time, difficulty or failure of some sort, they quickly complain that they don't have the favour of God, that God is not there and not helping them. Well, this was not true in the case of Joseph.

We can see God's favour throughout Joseph's life, both during the ups and downs. God's favour was always there to enable him to go through all the hardships and difficulties and come out victorious.

So, it is very clear that success is not only the outcome of what we do, sometimes the result of what we do is not a good indication of success. The true success is that His presence goes with you and that you know He is with you in what you do. it is His presence that gives us success.

Success is God's presence with you in what you do and it is doing God's will, doing the right thing at the right time in the right place in God's eyes, according to His heavenly pattern.

Joseph trusted God in all situations, no matter if he was up or down in his life. He stood firm in his belief and trusted in God alone.

You can have the favour of God and success in everything. Whether you are low in beginning or high in beginning, it does not matter; if the favour of God is in your life, His presence will go with you, even when you are in the lowest point of your life.

So often when we are in the lowest point of life, we think, we are a failure, we are no good, useless. Well, it does not matter what situation you are in, the most important thing is you have the favour of God and His presence goes with you.

PERSONAL EXPERIENCE

About seven years ago, my wife and I went to the USA to attend a meeting called The Lakeland Revival meeting. It lasted for a few months and was broadcast on the God channel. Many people from all around the world went to the meeting, eagerly seeking God. My wife and I went there, hungering for God, wanting to see God. It was awesome to see so many people hunger for God and His presence was so tangible in the meeting. It was the highest point of our spiritual lives.

On our return from the USA, my wife did not feel very well.

She went to see the doctor. The doctor referred her to the hospital. She had a 'check- up' and a scan to find out what was wrong. After the hospital had taken some tests we waited for the results. One week later we were back at the hospital to hear the results. It was such a crucial moment for us and the waiting was not easy at all. Waiting for the results felt like judgement day to me. My mind was thinking life or death.

When the consultant told us, "Your wife has cancer." That was the most scary word. No one would want to hear that word. The word 'cancer' hit us just like a bomb dropping on your head. You don't know what to do. We sat there motionless, speechless. Then, after a few seconds, we came back to our senses. I thought I heard incorrectly, and I asked the consultant again, "are you sure it is cancer?" I was hoping she would say otherwise but her answer was so firm, it was cancer. I turned to my wife and I told her "you have cancer." She took it very calmly with no tears in her eyes, no bitterness or no complaint at all, she was just so strong. She simply said two words, "trust God," and I praised God for her faith.

I asked the consultant what we should do now, what was the next step? She said my wife needed an operation and that the operation date would be after three months. "Three months?" I asked. The consultant looked me in the eyes and I looked at her. I prayed in my heart, Lord, that we find favour in your eyes. Then, suddenly, the consultant asked the nurse to give her the daily schedule. She asked the nurse who was on the list for the next week's operations. She looked at the daily, then looked at me, and asked the nurse to put my wife's name on the list for an operation that week. She asked my wife, "Can you come next week?" My wife said, "Yes." It was the favour of God, otherwise she would have to have waited for three months to have operation.

When the day of the operation came, I took my wife to hospital. It was a difficult moment, me and my wife sitting in the car before she went into the hospital. A lot of things were going through my mind. Would this be the last minute I saw my wife? Would she come out alive? What if she didn't make it? I suddenly felt so lonely. It seemed like there was no one else in the world, that I was the only person on earth, so lonely and in a deep valley of life. It seemed like I was in another world. I was having deep thoughts about life. What is life? Life is so short on this earth. I had all the memories of me and my wife and of our days together. At that time, we had been married for 27 years. We had lived happily together, had a good and successful marriage, and I didn't want it to end like this.

I did not know how my wife felt at that time. She was a strong woman of God. Before she went into the hospital for the operation, she said three words I will never forget. They were the three most important and humbling words in her life. She said, "Pray for me." It was the most difficult and lowest time of our lives. It was a time that really tested the strength of our faith and how firmly we were rooted in Jesus.

We examined ourselves; we searched our hearts, and asked ourselves have we sinned against God? Have we done anything wrong? Have we done anything outside of God's will that would cause this sickness to come upon my wife? But we soon realised it was the attack of the enemy against us. We then understood it was a spiritual warfare and we got ready to against it!

One thing we were absolutely one hundred percent certain about is that our God is a good God, and He is the God of love. He is our heavenly father, His love endures forever. We trust God to have a great plan in our lives. God is good all the time. When we were at the lowest point in our lives, when my wife was ill, we just took it as it came. We took it naturally. We did not say any negative words or complain about the situation and we never blamed anyone. We never complained to God about anything or doubted Him. We trust Him with all our heart, no matter what the outcome was, life or death. We were determined to trust Him. We thanked Him for His strength. When we look back at the situation we were in at the time, we wonder how we overcame all the difficulties we faced. Surely, it was the Holy Spirit who gave us such faith to trust God.

So he said to me, "This is the word of the Lord to Zerubbabel: 'Not by might nor by power, but by my Spirit,' says the Lord Almighty. ***(Zechariah 4:6)***

Praise the Lord; it is all about His favour within our lives. He brought us through a very difficult time and I have a personal understanding that we can experience His presence in all circumstances. Thank God my wife is now completely healed by His grace. We have come to know Him better than before through all the challenges.

I like what Job said; My ears had heard of you but now my eyes have seen you. ***(Job 42:5)***

No matter what circumstance or situation you are in, whether you are sick or in financial difficulty, having relationship problems or family issues, the most important thing is that you have the favour of God. His presence is with you and He has a good plan in your life. Often we may not know or understand why certain things are happening to us, or around us. Just like Joseph who did not understand why he was still in prison for the crime he did not commit.

He was wondering what was going on in his life. But I want to encourage you, because God knows everything that is going on in all of our lives. Because He created us in His own image and likeness, His eyes saw our unformed body. All of our days have been ordained for us, they were written in His book before we were even formed in our mothers' womb. He watches closely everything that happens in our lives, and we need to trust Him in all of our situations, just like Joseph trusted God in all circumstances.

Declare that you have the favour of God and whatever you do will be prosper and successful. Let the Spirit of success comes into your life now.

His presence is our success.

Chapter 4
God's Favour brings you promotion

Esther

Esther won the favour from the person responsible in the matter, which was Hegai.

She pleased him and won his favor. Immediately he provided her with her beauty treatments and special food. He assigned to her seven female attendants selected from the king's palace and moved her and her attendants into the best place in the harem. **(Esther 2:9)**

When the turn came for Esther (the young woman Mordecai had adopted, the daughter of his uncle Abihail) to go to the king, she asked for nothing other than what Hegai, the king's eunuch who was in charge of the harem, suggested. And Esther won the favor of everyone who saw her. 16 She was taken to King Xerxes in the royal residence in the tenth month, the month of Tebeth, in the seventh year of his reign. 17 Now the king was attracted to Esther more than to any of the other women, and she won his favor and approval more than any of the other virgins. So he set a royal crown on her head and made her queen instead of Vashti. ***(Esther 2:15-17)***

Following the advice of his wise man Memucan the king chose a new queen to take Vashti's place. Esther was taken to the King's palace and entrusted to Hegai.

She found favour and thus received special treatment. Esther received beauty treatments and special food, because of the favour of God; she later won the king's favour that resulted in her elevation and promotion to be queen.

Joseph

As we explored in the previous chapter, Joseph was promoted by Potiphar, then by the prison warden and finally promoted by Pharaoh.

After two years, he was brought out from prison to interpret a dream for Pharaoh, who knew of Joseph's ability and that God was with him. Pharaoh had no other person better than Joseph and appointed him to be second- in-command of the country. He was promoted by Pharaoh to be in charge of the whole land of Egypt. This was God's favour and a God given promotion.

Then Pharaoh said to Joseph, "Since God has made all this known to you, there is no one so discerning and wise as you. You shall be in charge of my palace, and all my people are to submit to your orders. Only with respect to the throne will I be greater than you." So Pharaoh said to Joseph, "I hereby put you in charge of the whole land of Egypt." Then Pharaoh took his signet ring from his finger and put it on Joseph's finger. He dressed him in robes of fine linen and put a gold chain around his neck. He had him ride in a chariot as his second-in-command, and people shouted before him, "Make way!" Thus he put him in charge of the whole land of Egypt. Then Pharaoh said to Joseph, "I am Pharaoh, but without your word no one will lift hand or foot in all Egypt." **(Genesis 41:39-44)**

No one from the east or the west or from the desert can exalt themselves. It is God who judges: He brings one down, he exalts another. **(Psalm 75:6-7)**

The favour of God can promote you to another level. Even though you may think you don't have the ability or qualifications to be promoted and stand no chance to be promoted in your situation, but look at the life of Joseph, He was in prison, it seemed there was no way out and that it was an impossible situation, and yet he was promoted to second- in –command of the country. You might be like that, in a hopeless situation and dreaming of promotion. When you have the favour of God, God can turn your hopeless situation around.

Promotion as the Bible says is not from the south, north or east, it is from God. It is Him alone who promotes people; it is Him alone who raises people up from the dust, to sit with the princes.

When God's favour comes to you, it can change everything. Gods' favour can change your whole life immediately.

For his anger lasts only a moment, but his favor lasts a lifetime; weeping may stay for the night, but rejoicing comes in the morning. ***(Psalm 30:5)***

All the examples we have seen so far in the book have been a direct result of the favour of God.

When the favour God comes to our life and promotion comes in the midst of difficulties, our attitude and responses also plays an important part when we face hardship, challenges or difficulty. Sometimes people have a misconception of Gods' favour. They think that when people have the favour of God in their lives, it means everything will go well and smoothly, that they will not experience any difficulties, face temptation, or be tested. Well, that is not true, When we looked at the life of Joseph, while indeed he had the favour of God, he encountered many difficulties in life. he still had to face testing and temptation. He was not exempt from temptation or trials of life.

In our response to the difficulties we face, our attitude and behaviour are important. Our promotion depends on our attitude. How high you want to go, depends on your attitude. Promotion is just around the corner; God is waiting to upgrade you and promote you to another level. So often we complain when we face hardship and things are not coming on the way we think they should be. Well, I think it is better to ask God to help us overcome our difficulties, instead of complaining about them. Then, we see promotion is coming our way. Favour is coming to us.

He called down famine on the land and destroyed all their supplies of food; and he sent a man before them—Joseph, sold as a slave. They bruised his feet with shackles, his neck was put in irons, till what he foretold came to pass, till the word of the Lord proved him true. ***(Psalm 105:16-19)***

In all this you greatly rejoice, though now for a little while you may have had to suffer grief in all kinds of trials. These have come so that the proven genuineness of your faith—of greater worth than gold, which perishes even though refined by fire—may result in praise, glory and honor when Jesus Christ is revealed. ***(1 Peter 1:6-7)***

We can learn so much from Joseph and his unwavering trust in God, despite all of the ups and downs in his life. He still served people, interpreted dreams for the prisoners and still honoured and revered God.

Throughout the scripture we do not see any bitterness or complaint in his heart, his integrity helped him remain triumphant throughout his situations. He came out victorious. He passed all the tests of life. We too, will face difficulty in life, testing will come. Sometimes our testing comes when we at the lowest point in life, but God will use all of the circumstance we are facing to see if we still trust in Him.

Promotion comes if we pass the test. All of the tests Joseph went through proved he was still trusting God and fear God.

Joseph took God seriously, he really meant business with God; he was a God fearer. Joseph himself confessed that he was a God fearer: On the third day, Joseph said to them, "Do this and you will live, for I fear God. (Genesis 42:18)

He always acknowledged the Lord ***(Genesis 40:8; 41:16).***

Pharaoh also testified that Joseph was special, because he had the Spirit of the Lord. **(Genesis 41:38)**

When he was tempted day after day, He was determined not to do any wicked thing and sin against God; he refused to go to bed with his master's wife or even to be with her.

No one is greater in this house than I am. My master has withheld nothing from me except you, because you are his wife. How then could I do such a wicked thing and sin against God?" And though she spoke to Joseph day after day, he refused to go to bed with her or even be with her. **(Genesis 39:9-10)**

When we started our church, we did not have our own place. We began by renting a hall to conduct the worship service and moved from place to place so many times.

At that time, we would conduct three services each Sunday in three different locations. It was very exhausting for us to run from place to place each Sunday and manpower became a concern. We always wanted to have a place of our own so that we could base ourselves in one location. We prayed and asked God to provide, but we still did not have any success in finding our own place.

One day we saw a potential venue in Chinatown. We tried to find out the Landlords' contact information but did not have any success. After a period of time, we found out that the place was under offer to another Christian organisation. As a result we did not pursue the matter further. However, one and a half years later and this place was still empty. Out of curiosity, we tried again to obtain the Landlady's information but as before, we did not have any connections. This time God sent us a person who was eager to help us, and finally we were connected to the Landlady

When we met the landlady the first thing she asked was, "Are you from the same organisation that we did not want to rent it to?" I replied, " No." Then she looked at me and said we want to rent the property to you. She did not even really know who I was and did not ask for any references at all. This was definitely the favour of God.

The property had been empty for such a long time and was already under offer to others, but the favour of God can change anything.

Finally, we have a venue right in the heart of Chinatown, where we now hold our Sunday services. God promoted our church and answered our prayers. We went from hiring a hall every week to having our own place. It was the favour of God.

God's favour takes you to another level, imagine yourself now being promoted to a higher position.

FAVOUR BRINGS YOU PROMOTION.

Chapter 5
God's favour connects you to your destiny

Ruth

Ruth was a poor Moabite, her husband died young, and she followed her mother in law Naomi back to her hometown Jerusalem. She picked up the leftover grain in the field.

And Ruth the Moabite said to Naomi, "Let me go to the fields and pick up the leftover grain behind anyone in whose eyes I find favor." **(Ruth 2:2)**

Later in her story she became connected to Boaz, eventually becoming the great grandmother of King David. She became the wife of Boaz, and that was her destiny. Even though the death of her husband was a sad tragedy God used this situation for her to meet and marry Boaz. The favour of God connected her to her destiny.

Joseph

We have spoken about Joseph a lot in our previous chapters, but his story contains so much depth that it requires our attention. Like Ruth, God used Josephs' hardships and difficulties to connect him with his destiny.

Despite all the hardship he had gone through, Joseph never doubted the dreams that God gave him. The dreams that he shared with his brothers that caused him to be sold into slavery, he could never forget the dreams, even though he was in prison, he never gave up hope, he never doubted God.

He treasured the dreams that God had given him when he was a young boy, he never forgot. Joseph trusted God to fulfil His words.

When God gives us a dream we should be like Joseph and never give up hope. When God gives us a prophetic word that speaks to our destiny, that speaks to our calling, or that speaks to our future we must keep it in our heart. So often the prophetic words that we have received are cast aside or forgotten. Gods' promises to us are YES and AMEN, they will come to pass. When we receive a dream or word from the Lord that speaks to our destiny, we need to treasure it in our hearts.

Don't let it get away, don't let other people discourage you, and don't let the devil steal it away from you. The enemy comes to steal, kill and destroy, that is his job. He comes to steal your dreams away, steal your destiny away. We need to hold on to our destiny and keep it in sight at all times. We can keep the dream alive by envisioning and speaking it to life.

Too often we allow ourselves to be discouraged by what others say. And too often we even allow ourselves to be discouraged by our own thoughts.

PERSONAL EXPERIENCE

When I first became a Christian, during one of the Sunday services a boy had a vision that he saw me. He said I was standing on the platform and Jesus was there on the platform standing beside me. The boy was so excited and came to tell me about the vision, but at that time I did not know what the vision really meant. Nevertheless I too felt excited, because Jesus was there with me.

Even though I did not fully understand the meaning; I knew in my heart, that it was my destiny to become a Pastor. I knew that it was my calling and I knew that one day I would be speaking in the church. I began to share the vision with people and one of the sisters discouraged and rebuked me. She accused me of being too proud because I wanted to be a pastor.

I felt so discouraged because of what she said to me, it was like a bucket of cold water pouring over my head. The embarrassment I felt caused me to want to hide my face so that no one would see me. I thought she would encourage me and say good things, but she only brought condemnation.

In spite of this I knew what my dream and destiny was. I prayed to God, telling Him about the dream, telling him about my desire. I trusted in Him and continued to imagine myself preaching to many people. I was always dreaming about it.

Well, God is good because He has a good plan for our lives, He wants you to fulfil the destiny that He has planned for you. Don't let go of whatever He has shown you in your dreams, don't let go of your destiny. It is the favour of God that will connect you to your destiny.

God has a good plan for each one of our lives. He favour us, He will connect us with the right people and He will enable us to fulfil our destinies.

God connected Ananias with Paul, and also connected Barnabas too. God connected them to enable Paul to fulfil his destiny. God's favour connected them.

God usually brings people into our lives for a purpose. He often uses our circumstances to connect us to the right people who will propel us further forward. If you are reading this book and having difficulty meeting the right people please don't be discouraged. God sees our every move and answers every prayer. He is a faithful and just God. He began a good work in us and He will bring it into completion. God commits Himself to finish everything He starts.

When you have the favour of God in your life, God will connect you to the right person, in the right place and at a right time. When I wrote my first book, hearing God's voice, I never dreamed or imagined that I would write a book. The favour of God connected me to the right person, in the right place. It was through that person and his encouragement that I wrote my first book. It was a divine connection, it is God's favour in my life.

Many years ago, I was invited by an organisation to an event called Global Day of Prayer. They invited me to say a prayer at the West Ham football stadium; it was a big event that attracted several thousands of people. At that time I was a young Christian church worker, and was not well known. In fact not many people knew me. Maybe to some of you reading this book, saying a prayer in a big meeting is not very important or significant to you. As I was new to the Christian circle I treasured that moment, it was significant in the spiritual realm. From that event I knew God was doing something special in my life.

So often we neglect the things that are happening in our lives and don't pay attention. God is always working on our behalf, and we need to be mindful and view things from a spiritual perspective. We must use both our physical and spiritual eyes to observe what is happening around us. Sometimes when these unusual things happen in our lives it is an indication that something is moving in the spiritual realm. When we experience the move of God in our lives, we need to thank God for all He does. I knew in my heart something was happening in the heavenly realm, I thank God for His favour, and that He chose me to pray at that event.

A few years ago, I received an invitation to go to Downing Street for an Easter reception. When I first received the invitation, I thought it must have been fake. The invitation read Bobby Sung, and at first I just ignored it. When I looked at it again and again, I asked myself, am I dreaming? I was not convinced that the invitation was genuine but I decided to reply.

I said to myself, let me reply to them, since there was no harm in replying, if it is not from Downing Street, I have nothing to lose, if it is from them, then I am very happy.

The invitation stated I should bring my passport with me to verify my identification. They had invited me as Bobby Sung but my real name is Y.K Sung, I explained the matter and asked them if they could issue me with another invitation with my real name. I waited for their reply to see if the invitation was real or fake. They replied immediately and sent me another invitation card with my real name on it. I know it definitely wasn't a dream; it was the real invitation from Downing Street to invite me to attend the Easter reception.

As I said before, I was not well known, I thought they must have mixed up my name with another person's name, but whatever it was, God never makes mistake. It was the favour of God that took me to that place.

God always has a good plan for each of our lives, even though it may not always appear that way. He will work it out in His own way, in His own time. He will connect you with the right people, and bring them alongside you to assist you in fulfilling your destiny. Continue to trust Him and never give up hope. Don't lose sight of your destiny and keep your dream alive just as Joseph did.

Remember our God is God of favour, He loves to favour you. He is longing to pour out His favour into your life.

GOD'S FAVOUR CONNECTS YOU TO YOUR DESTINY.

Chapter 6
God's favour brings you financial breakthrough

Abraham

Abraham received the favour of God, and God promised to bless him.

"I will make you into a great nation, and I will bless you; I will make your name great, and you will be a blessing. I will bless those who bless you, and whoever curses you I will curse; and all peoples on earth will be blessed through you. ***(Genesis 12:2-3)***

But the land could not support them while they stayed together, for their possessions were so great that they were not able to stay together. ***(Genesis 13:6)***

Abraham had a financial breakthrough, God blessed him in the beginning of Genesis chapter 12 and in the same chapter he received wealth from

Pharaoh, and after that in chapter 13, we see his wealth, he had so many livestock, silver and gold. He was so wealthy because of the favour of God in his life. God was the source of his riches.

Isaac

In **(Genesis 26:1)** we see that Isaac planted crops in that land, but famine occurred in the same year. Nevertheless he still reaped a hundred fold. Everywhere was affected by the famine and the people had nothing to eat, it was an impossible situation. Despite this he was still successful, not only did he plant crops, he also dug wells.

The enemy Philistines filled the wells with dirt in an attempt to prevent him digging. Isaac continued and reopened the well that his father Abraham had dug. However the enemy's herdsmen quarrelled with his herdsmen each time. In spite of this Isaac kept on digging the well and was successful.

Even his enemy asked him to leave because they saw the presence of God and God's blessing upon Isaac's life, (Genesis 26:28-29) they answered, "We saw clearly that the LORD was with you. And now you are blessed by the LORD."

As we can see whatever Isaac did, he was successful. In the year of famine, because of the favour of God, Isaac still prospered in whatever he did. Despite what the situation was, he still had financial breakthrough.

Joseph

Joseph stored up huge quantities of grain, like the sand of the sea; it was so much that he stopped keeping records because it was beyond measure. ***(Genesis 41:49)***

When the famine had spread over the whole country, Joseph opened all the storehouses and sold grain to the Egyptians, for the famine was severe throughout Egypt. ***(Genesis 41:56)***

So Joseph bought all the land in Egypt for Pharaoh. The Egyptians, one and all, sold their fields, because the famine was too severe for them. The land became Pharaoh's, ***(Genesis 47:20)***

Joseph was sold as a slave and ended up in Egypt, but years later it was he who took total control of the wealth of the whole nation. He was in charge of the country's economy and the entire wealth of the nation was in his hands. What a supernatural financial breakthrough it was!

The favour of God was surely in his life, even though there was famine everywhere, no food, and no production. In fact in the three examples I mentioned above, Abraham, Isaac and Joseph, they all lived in a time of famine. Pharaoh gave sheep and cattle, male and female donkeys, men servants, maidservants and camels to Joseph. Abraham became very rich, (Genesis 12:16) Isaac became very rich too. Abimelech told him to leave them and Joseph became very wealthy from the nation. They all sold their lands to him, and he collected all the wealth for Pharaoh (Genesis 47:14; 47:20-21).

In times of difficult financial situation, we all need the favour of God. The world is a very uncertain place, but no matter how bad our circumstances are, we can still succeed and have breakthrough in what we do. When God's favour is upon our life, God makes us different to the world, we belong to God, we are His people.

As God said to Moses in (Exodus 8), He will separate the Israelites and Egyptians. They are different. Israel and Egypt are different. Israel represents God's people and Egypt represents the world.

*"But on that day I will deal differently with the land of Goshen, where my people live; no swarms of flies will be there, so that you will know that I, the Lord, am in this land. (**Exodus 8:22**)*

But the LORD will make a distinction between the livestock of Israel and that of Egypt, so that no animal belonging to the Israelites will die.'" **(Exodus 9:4)**

God's favour in our life brings financial breakthrough, because our God is a generous God, and He loves to give us the best. He supplies all our needs, as the psalmist said: *I was young and now I am old, yet I have never seen the righteous forsaken or their children begging bread. (**Psalm 37:25**)* also in **(Philippians 4:19)** And my God will meet all your needs according to His glorious riches in Christ Jesus. And also in the book of **Ephesians 3:20** *Now to Him who is able to do immeasurably more than all we ask or imagine, according to His power that is at work within us.*

Our God will give us more than we could ever ask or imagine. If we have the favour of God working in our life, we don't need to worry about our needs. As our Lord Jesus said, look at the birds of the air and the lilies of the field, they don't sow and they don't reap, yet my God supplies all their needs.

God always supplies all our needs, we need to be faithful in small things then God will surely give us the big things. We must learn to be good stewards as Joseph was.

Let me share with you, on one occasion many years ago, when I was a new Christian, I received money from people in my local church. After a Sunday service, someone gave me a cheque, for fifty pounds. The person told me that it was from God and that God had told them to give it to me. When I received it, I said to myself, "I don't need money, God you made a mistake or maybe that person made a mistake." Afterwards I prayed about it and asked what He wanted me to do with the money. After praying God showed me a sister who was serving in the mission field, so I gave the money to her.

Don't overlook the small things, to some of us fifty pounds seems small, but to another person fifty pounds could be a lot more. One blessing can lead to more blessings; it all depends on how you manage your money. So often we don't take care of the small things, but God sees our hearts. We all have accounts in heaven. *As Paul said: Not that I desire your gifts; what I desire is that more be credited to your account.* ***(Philippians 4:17)***

When you manage money well, God will release more financial seeds to you, so that you can continue to sow. God wants us to scatter the blessings throughout His kingdom with the seeds that He places in our hands.

We use what we have to bless people. Don't let the blessing stop at you. Sow a seed into someone else's life, when you keep sowing you will keep reaping.

Our God is the supplier of all the resources we have. Every good gift is from Him alone. Jesus is our perfect example, He never lacked any thing, God the Father provided all of his needs. Because he was the Son of man and God favoured him. He was never without the things that he needed. When the people only had 5 loaves of bread and two fishes, God enabled a miracle that resulted in five thousand people being fed. What a breakthrough! Pay attention on what you have and be a good steward, you will see the favour of God working in your life.

The favour of God in your life will make a noticeable difference, His favour will bring you financial breakthrough.

I remember a time when my car's exhaust pipe was broken and needed fixing. When I brought it to the garage, I was ready to pay the bill but the manager said, "Oh, I remember you, you had your car exhaust pipe replaced few years ago, it's free this time." It surely was the favour of God.

I could not even remember having my car repaired a few years ago and even though it was not so much money for a replacement of a car exhaust pipe, it was the favour of God that caused the garage manager not to charge me.

It may seem insignificant but it always leads to a bigger breakthrough. Pay attention to your small breakthroughs, give thanks to Him and praise Him for small things.

God wants to see if we will be a good steward of small breakthroughs or not, if we are faithful in small things then He will give us greater things, that is what Jesus said in Matthew chapter 25:23, *"you have been faithful with a few things, I will put you in charge of many things."*

One of my colleagues and his family moved from Hong Kong to the UK several years ago. He came to my church for full time ministry. One of the things he had to sort out for his family was to find a suitable accommodation. They decided to sell their apartment in Hong Kong and buy a house here in the UK. They were looking for a house with three bedrooms, but they didn't have enough money for that. One day a property agent called him about a property with a very good price, but the agent also told him that there was another person who had already given an offer on the property.

After a month, the property agent called my colleague again saying that the property was still available. For some reason the landlord seemed unable to complete the sale. Finally my colleague brought that property and it was one hundred thousand pounds lower than the market value. It really was God's favour for him.

Actually the property was empty for a year and had not been put on market until my colleague arrived in the UK. They didn't have enough money to buy the property, and they prayed to God for a house with three bedrooms, but they finally got one with four bedrooms. This is

God's great provision and financial breakthrough. The favour of God was in his life.

THE FAVOUR OF GOD MAKES EVERYTHING DIFFERENT AND BRINGS YOU FINANCIAL BREAKTHROUGH. DECLARE THAT YOU ARE WEALTHY. YOU HAVE THE FAVOUR OF GOD.

Chapter 7
Position yourself

We need to engage in God's favour in order to experience the fullness of it.

In the last chapter, I have shown you that God has chosen us for His favour, and how the favour of God works in people's lives. Yes! God's favour is ready for all of us.

The question is why are there so many, even Christians, who are yet to experience God's favour fully as promised in the Bible? They may know about God's favour but they have never engaged in it to receive all the blessing available to them.

So I am going to share with you three principles for engaging yourself in God's favour. First, you have to position yourself for God's favour. Second, you have to set your mind to tune in with God's favour. Third, you have to speak the positive words and claim your favour.

For example if you want Italian food, you need to locate an Italian restaurant and go inside. If you want Chinese food, you need to locate a Chinese restaurant and go inside. In the same way, we need to locate the real source of favour and position ourselves alongside it to receive God's favour. People go all around the world looking for different religions or go to different places looking for blessing through idols. They will not get a blessing, because they are positioned at the wrong place.

The only way we can receive the full measure of God's favour is to position ourselves in Jesus, for He is the ultimate source of all God's favour. The Bible says in the gospel of John: *The Word became flesh and made his dwelling among us. We have seen his glory, the glory of the one and only Son, who came from the Father, full of grace and truth.* ***(John 1:14)***

Grace and favour are just two different translations for the same Greek word. Here it says Jesus is full of favour [or grace] and truth. Jesus Himself is the favour [or grace] from the Father. Jesus embodies all God's favour and lives among us.

Jesus came to proclaim the year of the Lord's favour.

He went to Nazareth, where he had been brought up, and on the Sabbath day he went into the synagogue, as was his custom. He stood up to read, and the scroll of the prophet Isaiah was handed to him. Unrolling it, he found the place where it is written: "The Spirit of the Lord is on me, because he has anointed me to proclaim good news to the poor. He has sent me to proclaim freedom for the prisoners and recovery of sight for the blind, to set the oppressed free, to proclaim the year of the Lord's favor." Then he rolled up the scroll, gave it back to the attendant and sat down. The eyes of everyone in the synagogue were fastened on him. ***(Luke 4:16-20)***

The passage Jesus read is in Isaiah 61:1-2. But Jesus did not finish reading the whole verse; he read only the first part of verse 2 and skipped the end of verse 3, which is about the day of vengeance of our God. Jesus intended to emphasise the first part of the verse, in order to highlight the year of our Lord's favour. *just as the Son of Man did not come to be served, but to serve, and to give his life as a ransom for many."* ***(Matthew 20:28)***

He came to serve, He gave His life as a ransom for many, He set the captives free, healed the sick, preached the good news to the poor. He came to die on the cross to release the favour of God to the whole world, by shedding His precious blood. Because of the cross, today is the day of salvation and acceptance.

As Paul later said in the book of Corinthians: If any of you has a dispute with another, do you dare to take it before the ungodly for judgment instead of before the Lord's people? 2 Or do you not know that the Lord's people will judge the world?

And if you are to judge the world, are you not competent to judge trivial cases? 3 Do you not know that we will judge angels? How much more the things of this life! **(2 Corinthians 6:1-3)**

Jesus came to proclaim the favour of God, and Paul reiterated this, Jesus' coming represented the time of favour. We have all received the favour of God, because of what Jesus did for us. He died on the cross because he loves us, and this enabled us to receive the favour of God.

Therefore, the first key to engage in God's favour is to receive salvation, only then will you have full legal rights and access. The Bible says,

Let us then approach God's throne of grace with confidence, so that we may receive mercy and find grace to help us in our time of need. **(Hebrews 4:16)**

See, you have access to "the throne of grace [same Greek word for 'grace' and 'favour']" and 'find favour' in Jesus. Without Jesus, you are unable to connect to God's favour. But with Jesus, you have every good thing from heaven. With Jesus, you are positioned before "the throne of favour".

David was definitely a God-favoured person, he declared with the revelation of the Holy Spirit,

I say to the Lord, "You are my Lord; apart from you I have no good thing." **(Psalm 16:2)**

David correctly recognised and honoured God. He acknowledged that his favour was from the Lord. He knew how to always position himself when he needed to receive God's favour. We must recognise that salvation and favour are linked, to position is to put yourself in relation to something or someone. To position yourself in favour, you have to position yourself as a child of God, through believing in Jesus.

This new identity in Jesus is your full assurance to receive all of God's favour. Your identity will be changed from a slave in the world to a child of God, because of Jesus. A slave always struggles for favour, because they have no freedom at all. Trying to work hard and please their master, hoping their master will favour them and not treat them too harshly.

In contrast, a child does not need to struggle for favour from a loving Father, because it is about our relationship. Father God loves His children.

Every good and perfect gift is from above, coming down from the Father of the heavenly lights, who does not change like shifting shadows. ***(James 1:17)***

Our Father in heaven is ready to pour out His favour upon His children.

BECOME A CHILD OF GOD

When we repent of our sin and accept Jesus as our Lord and Saviour, we became the children of God, adopted into His family.

*Yet to all who did receive him, to those who believed in his name, he gave the right to become children of God— **(John 1:12)***

*He predestined us for adoption to sonship through Jesus Christ, in accordance with his pleasure and will— **(Ephesians 1:5)***

If you believe Jesus and accept Him as your Lord and saviour, you will have the favour of God in you. The Grace of God will come in to your life.

We have the birth right to receive God's favour, because we were born to have the favour of God, we were made in the image of God, God created everything good, and He saw it was very good. You were created by God, and when He saw you He was pleased.

In fact when God created us, He crowned us with glory and honour.

*You have made them a little lower than the angels and crowned them with glory and honor. **(Psalm 8:5)***

We were prepared in advance for glory.

What if he did this to make the riches of his glory known to the objects of his mercy, whom he prepared in advance for glory— ***(Romans 9:23)***

RESTORATION OF GOD'S FAVOUR

When Adam sinned against God, man became a fallen race, falling short of the glory of God.

Jesus came to die on the cross, He represented the whole human race to die on the cross and shed his precious blood to redeem us. All He had accomplished on the cross, all the blessings, all the favour in Him now belongs to us. Because of what Jesus had done on the cross we can access the favour of God. Not because of what we have done, not because we obey the law, not because of our own merit, not through our own ability. No! It is all by the grace of God. We were saved by grace, not by work, so that no one can boast.

Indeed we were saved by the grace of God not by our own work. It is all about the finished work of Jesus. We can inherit all the blessing.

I always thank my God for you because of his grace given you in Christ Jesus. 5 For in him you have been *enriched in every way—with all kinds of speech and with all knowledge—***(1 Corinthians 1:4-5)**

For it is by grace you have been saved, through faith—and this is not from yourselves, it is the gift of God—not by works, so that no one can boast. ***(Ephesians 2:8-9)***

The Bible clearly tells us that we received grace and favour from Jesus. According to Ephesian 2:8-9, it is by grace and not by works.

Let us look at the book of Ephesians chapter one. Praise be unto God and father of our Lord Jesus Christ, who blessed us in the heavenly realm with every spiritual blessings in Christ. He blessed us with all spiritual blessings. The Bible here used past tense for verbs, which means He has already blessed us; it is done already, not just one blessing, not just earthly blessings or material blessings but every spiritual blessing, that also includes earthly and heavenly blessings.

Ephesians chapter one also talks about sonship, in verse five the scripture says "He predestined us to be adopted as his sons through Jesus Christ, in accordance with his pleasure and will."

All the blessing belongs to you if you are a child of God, because you become a co-heir with Christ.

Now if we are children, then we are heirs—heirs of God and co-heirs with Christ, if indeed we share in his sufferings in order that we may also share in his glory. ***(Romans 8:17)***

It is yours, favour in your family, favour in your business, favour in your church, favour will overtake you wherever you go.

Paul understood the grace of God, he said:

But by the grace of God I am what I am, and his grace to me was not without effect. No, I worked harder than all of them—yet not I, but the grace of God that was with me. ***(1 Corinthians 15:10)***

I thank Christ Jesus our Lord, who has given me strength, that he considered me trustworthy, appointing me to his service. 13 Even though I was once a blasphemer and a persecutor and a violent man, I was shown mercy because I acted in ignorance and unbelief. 14 The grace of our Lord was poured out on me abundantly, along with the faith and love that are in Christ Jesus. ***(1 Timothy 1:12-14)***

Paul received the grace of God, he became who he was. He received favour upon favour in his life.

NO MORE STRUGGLES

We don't need to struggle to get God's favour and we don't need to be envious about our neighbour's favour. You can have the favour of God in your own life, because you believe in Jesus.

Abraham's blessing is yours, all that Jesus has is yours, Jesus is full of grace and truth. When you receive Jesus into your life, you receive grace, you have the favour of God in your life.

What a wonderful truth, we need to understand that we have the favour of God, you don't need to struggle to have the favour of God, what you need is to realise you already have the favour of God.

Sometimes people try to earn the favour of God by their own good works, in the end they become discouraged, they give up, and in the end they blame God. They wonder what is wrong with them because the word of God says, we have the favour of God, and somehow they don't seem to experience the favour of God in their life.

The problems do not lie in the truth that we have heard, but how we respond to the truth of God's favour. People will respond differently according to their faith in God, this is why some get it and some do not get it. Just like what Jesus illustrates in Mark 4, God's words were sown like seeds, "some fell along the path," which means they did not receive the truth at all. "Some fell on rocky places," which means they only received the truth superficially but without root in their hearts. Some were 'choked' by 'thorns,' which means that they do not produce fruit. Only those, like good soil, who have faith to receive the truth and treasure it and hold fast to it will produce fruits.

Many have heard about God's favour, but they don't receive it at all. They leave the truth outside, "along the path," and let satan come and take it away. Some receive it superficially, without taking root in Jesus, like those who "fell on rocky places." These two types of people do not position themselves to receive God's favour. This is why they don't get it.

For those choked by the "thorns" they are struggling to receive God's favour because they put focus on a worldly standard. They think they have to obey all regulations and receive God's favour by merit, No. As I said earlier we obey God because we love Him not to earn favour. Only those who position themselves purely in Jesus will be fruitful in receiving God's favour. They receive the truth completely and have faith in Jesus only.

How we understand truth is important, some people don't believe it in their hearts, they just believe in their head, there is a big difference between the head and the heart.

When you believe in your head, you can understand it but with no effect. For example we all received the grace and favour of God, we all received the truth but some people are still very miserable. Some still have no evidence of the favour of God, because they do not believe it or they try to earn it. Because of this, the grace of God is not effective in their life.

The favour of God can work mightily in our lives, if we activate it. You may say what do you mean by activate it? What I mean is, put it into action. Believe that you have the favour of God and declare it. We will talk more about this in our next chapter.

When we look at our lives, we should be so thankful to God, because He has blessed us so much. He has blessed us with so many things, we have received salvation, we have received the gifts, all that we have, all the many resources He has given to us. We have all received the favour of God.

YOU HAVE THE FAVOUR OF GOD BECAUSE YOU ARE THE CHILDREN OF GOD.

Chapter 8
Change your Mind-set

When you go into a great restaurant, you are well positioned to try a great variety of good food, but you may choose to get many delicious dishes or only a glass of water. What you get depends on what you want. So, the next thing you have to do is to make up your mind. What do you want from the restaurant?

Like receiving God's favour, becoming a child of God is the first step to get you well positioned to receive God's royal treasure of favour. Next, you have to set your mind to expect good things from the heavenly Father. What you get depends on how you think. What we think about is important.

For as he thinks in his heart, so is he. **(Proverbs 23: 7)**

What we think in our heart will become who we are, if we think we are no good, we already projected ourselves to be no good. If we think we are useless, we will indeed become useless. The opposite is also true, if we think we are good, we will have a positive projection of ourselves. So if we think we are useful and valuable, then we will become useful and valuable.

This is how it works in the spiritual realm, and that is why our thinking is important to us, because it affects all areas of our lives. If we think we are blessed and that we are highly favoured, then the favour of God will come into our life.

THINK LIKE JESUS

Change your thinking: we need to have the mind of Christ and to think like Jesus.

"Who has known the mind of the Lord so as to instruct him?" But we have the mind of Christ. ***(1 Corinthians 2:16)***

Jesus' mind does not worry about tomorrow; He taught us in Matthew chapter 6:25-34 do not worry about tomorrow, for tomorrow will worry about itself. He told us to look at the birds of the air, they do not sow or reap or store away in barns, and yet our heavenly father feeds them, and then He said again, about the lilies of the field, how God the Father clothes them, so He said don't worry about tomorrow. Jesus's mind does not have any negative thoughts, we need to think like Jesus thinks.

*We demolish arguments and every pretension that sets itself up against the knowledge of God, and we take captive every thought to make it obedient to Christ.(**2 Corinthians 10:5**)*

No more thinking negatively. No more worrying about if you can achieve it. No more struggle and being jealous of other people's favour. You have your portion of favour so change your mind-set. Believe that you have the favour of God and you will receive the favour of God.

I receive the favour of God all the time, I still remember when my son applied for a place to study in secondary school sixth form, he was rejected because there were so many people who applied to the school. We were so disappointed that my son could not get into that school. At that time there were not many good schools in the location. What should we do? I said to God, "God I am your child, I have your favour and you love me."

After a while God spoke to me, He said wait for the good news. In my heart, I knew God was speaking to me, we had already planned to go out on bank holiday Monday, but I decided to cancel it at the last minute.

I knew in my heart that there were some good things about to happen. The phone rang on bank holiday Monday, it was from the school, they asked if we still wanted my son to go to their school. They said they could offer my son a place, my reply was "YES!" "The favour of God will turn failure into success." We were overjoyed.

It was the favour of God, even though it was initially a rejection, the favour of God turned things around. Here, once again, I learnt that having a positive mind-set and faith in God brings breakthrough to receive God's favour. God is able to turn around the rejection.

Therefore realise we have the favour of God and having a correct mind-set is very important.

As I said before favour is unmerited, we can't earn it, therefore we need to change our mind-set, and change the way we think. Think positively and expect great things from God.

When you expect good things to happen, they will happen. If you believe it, you will receive it.

Grace and peace be yours in abundance through the knowledge of God and of Jesus our Lord. ***(2 Peter 1:2)***

EXPECT FAVOUR OF GOD.

Position yourself to receive the favour of God every day. Expect good things to happen in your life, look on the bright side every day. Be cheerful! Every day is a new day that God has made especially for you.

When our mind is full of expectation of good things, it will change the spiritual atmosphere around us and attract God's favour comes into our lives.

King David was a favour minded person, he lived a life focused on God's favour. He expected God's favour to come upon his life all of the time, even when he did something terribly wrong. He took Uriah's wife Bathsheba and also murdered him, yet he still expected God's favour to come to him.

Surely your goodness and love will follow me all the days of my life, and I will dwell in the house of the Lord forever. ***(Psalm 23:6)***

Have expectations every day when you wake up. As a new day begins our heart should expect good things to happen. Favour will be increased, in 2 Peter 1:2 it said Grace and peace be yours in abundance. Through the knowledge of God and of Jesus our Lord.

That means an increase of God's favour in our lives, continuing to increase, every day there is an increase in favour.

If you have this kind of expectation, you will see a difference in your life. When you go out to meet people, the favour of God will just come upon your life. Everything you do will prosper, you wait for a bus and it will come at the right time. When you travel home, there will be no traffic jam, whatever you do, God's presence will be with you.

I live every day with positive expectations, I expect the favour of God. I expect God to give me a good and positive surprise, which He always does.

I remember last year when I went to hospital to visit people. I was very thirsty on my way to the hospital and my mouth became so dry. I was really thirsty! At that time I was on a bus, but I thought I can't wait until I get to the hospital. I decided to get off the bus half way to the hospital and buy a bottle of water.

After I bought the water I saw that the same bus was still at the bus stop. Then the bus driver made an announcement and said: "Sorry, the bus has to stop here for a few minutes". So, I boarded the same bus and continued my journey. The bus stopped for me to buy a bottle of water. That was the favour of God.

Expect the good things to happen in your life every day. Favour comes in different shapes and sizes, big and small.

On another occasion when I took a train home, I knew I was late. I didn't think it would be possible for me to catch the train. The time was quite late and I did not want to run. However, to my surprise, when I arrived at the station, the train was delayed by ten minutes, so I hadn't missed it. The train was waiting for me! The favour of God again! Always expect good things!

You may say to me, what about if I am sick? What about if I have no job? What about if I have financial difficulty? How can I expect good things?

Yes, you still can expect good things, we must live in expectation. For example if you have some kind of sickness, what is your expectation, you should expect to get better and be healed.

You may have a sickness, that may be your situation right now. But it does not have to be permanent, the fact of your sickness can be changed. You may be unwell in this moment but it may get better in next second, the sickness may suddenly disappear, you may be healed supernaturally.

But truth cannot be changed, the truth is from heaven and it stands firm in eternity. The truth says you are healthy. The truth says God will heal you because you are His child.

Your expectation is to believe the truth; the truth says you are healthy, so you are healthy.

Think positively, think you are healthy and expect good health. Every day you should think of good things and expect good things. When you do this you will get good things.

You may not have money, which may be a fact, but truth says all the blessings are yours. You will inherit the world, Abraham's blessing is yours, everything Jesus has is yours. We need to choose to expect the favour of God. The truth says I can have all of the blessings, and I will certainly have all the blessings.

Our expectation is very important. If we train ourselves to expect good things, we invite God to surprise us with wonderful blessings.

I'd like to share another testimony with you. Roughly over 10 years ago, I took a team with me to South Korea to join the prayer mountain conference. At the end of the conference on the last day there was a big banquet. Several thousand people attended the banquet and I sat with my church members. Before the dinner was served, I was invited to sit at the chairman's table. My initial reaction was to say "no thank you" as I didn't want to leave my church members. In the end I agreed and was taken to the chairman's table to sit with the chairman of Prayer Mountain, South Korea.

That was a pleasantly surprising experience as I genuinely did not expect to be sitting at the

Chairman's table. It was the favour of God. God will always surprise us with good things!

We live every day in the favour of God, we are special, God created us in His own image and He crowned us with honour and glory (Psalm 8).

We do not need to struggle to live life, Jesus promised us to have an abundant life, a full life. How can we have an abundant life if we don't have the favour of God. When you accept Jesus as your Lord and saviour, you can always have the favour of God working in your life.

Some people never expect good things to come into their life; they always think bad and negative thoughts. They believe they are not good enough to receive the favour of God, that they are unworthy. Their mind is full of negative thoughts. That type of thinking is destructive, and it is a lie from the enemy. You need to change your negative mind-set, train yourself to think differently, train yourself to think like Jesus. Expect good things to happen in your life and always remind yourself to have a positive mind-set.

CHANGE OUR MIND-SET. WE MUST HAVE THE MIND OF CHRIST.

Chapter 9
Speak the Right Words

I'd like to use a restaurant as an illustration as I did in the previous chapter. Once you locate the restaurant and decide what you want to eat, the next step is to order what you want. Your words are very important because you get what you order. In the same way, every word from our mouth is extremely crucial in receiving God's favour.

Yes we know, it is by grace alone and not by our own effort for us to receive favour. But we also have an important part to play. Although the favour of God belongs to us, God wants to bless us and favour us, we need to believe it and receive it. If we don't believe it, we won't receive it.

Even Jesus could not do anything while He was in His home town. The people did not believe Him, they said negative words about him, despised him. Therefore our words are important. Words carry power, when God created the heavens and the earth, He used His Word to create the heavens and the earth. We are made in the image of God, therefore what we say has power to create life or death.

Words have power (Proverb 18:21) the tongue has the power of life and death, and those who love it will eat its fruits.

The words we speak, come from our hearts, as Jesus said in (Matthew 15:18) *But the things that come out of a person's mouth come from the heart, and these defile them. For out of the heart come evil thoughts—murder, adultery, sexual immorality, theft, false testimony, slander.*

A good heart will speak good things and a bad heart will speak bad things. Whatever is inside of us is revealed by the words we speak. It is important that we speak the right words because it can affect the spiritual realm.

We can create a spiritual atmosphere of life or death around us, through what we speak. As written in the last part of Proverbs 18:21 and those who love it will eat its fruit. Just to reiterate, if we speak positive words we shall eat positive things, but if we speak negative words we shall eat negative things.

REFRAIN FROM NEGATIVE WORDS

Negative words will bring negative results, and even bring death. Negative speech is one of the many things that cut people off from God's favour. Therefore, we must refrain from speaking negatively in order to receive God's favour.

Life and death is in the power of the tongue, we have the ability to bless or curse ourselves based on what we say. When we complain, murmur and curse we displease God.

God wanted to take the people of Israel to the promise land, because they were His covenant people. God favoured them and choose them to be his people. God desired to give them the best of everything.

The people were complaining, gossiping and complaining about God, because there was no food or water. Their hearts were full of bitterness and unbelief. In Numbers 14:2 All the Israelites grumbled against Moses and Aaron, and the whole assembly said to them, "if only we had died in Egypt! Or in this desert!"

They said they were willing to die in the wilderness. Our words have power, and in the end, they died in the wilderness and failed to enter the promise land. In Number 26:64-65 not one of them were among those counted by Moses and Aaron the priest. When they counted the Israelites in the Desert of Sinai. For the Lord had told those Israelites that they would surely die in the desert, and not one of them was left except Caleb son of Jephunneh and Joshua son of Nun.

They all died in the wilderness, except for two people, Joshua and Caleb. They both believed in the word of God, and they had faith in God's word.

Be careful of your tongue, and the words you say. When we face hardship or difficulty we often speak quickly, we tend to say things that we ought not to say. No wonder in the book of James he tells us: My *dear brothers and sisters, take note of this: Everyone should be quick to listen, slow to speak and slow to become angry,* ***(James 1:19)***

SPEAK POSITIVE WORDS

Speak positive words to claim your favour.

Throughout this book we have examined how Joseph had the favour of God. We saw that when he was wrongly put into prison, sold as a slave by his brothers Joseph was not angry nor did he complain. He did not attempt to take revenge or harbour bitterness in his heart.

In the face of all the hardship and mistreatment, Joseph remained in right standing with God and maintained a humble attitude.

As stated in **1 Peter 3:9-10**: *Do not repay evil with evil or insult with insult. On the contrary, repay evil with blessing, because to this you were called so that you may inherit a blessing. For, "Whoever would love life and see good days must keep their tongue from evil and their lips from deceitful speech……."*

God destined us to have favour and blessing, we were called to inherit blessing and it belongs to us. However we must be careful of the words that proceed from our mouth. Jesus was oppressed and afflicted.

He was oppressed and afflicted, yet he did not open his mouth; he was led like a lamb to the slaughter, and as a sheep before its shearers is silent, so he did not open his mouth. ***(Isaiah 53:7)***

Jesus did not say a negative word, even when he was hung on the cross. He said: Jesus said, "Father, forgive them, for they do not know what they are doing." **(Luke 23:34)**

Let us look at Isaac; he was oppressed by the enemy Philistine. Isaac did not argue with them, he did not say a bad word about them, he did not say any negative words about himself, he just moved on. God blessed him one hundredfold.

It is very important that when we face injustice or difficult, hardship like Joseph that we do not speak negative words about ourselves or others, we need to let God deal with the matter, God said revenge is His.

When I first started the church, I did not have any experience in pastoring. Most of the leaders left the church shortly after it started. When they left only 15 to 18 people remained including my wife and I. It was a struggle, I was hurt, I was down, I was angry, but I kept myself from speaking negative words. I kept my heart clean and spoke well. And remembered what the Bible said: Do not repay anyone evil for evil.

Do not repay anyone evil for evil. Be careful to do what is right in the eyes of everyone. If it is possible, as far as it depends on you, live at peace with everyone. Do not take revenge, my dear friends, but leave room for God's wrath, for it is written: "It is mine to avenge; I will repay," says the Lord. **(Romans 12:17-19)**

Speak positive words, faith filled word. Be careful not to say negative things if you want the favour of God. Often we say things we don't mean, for example: when Chinese people sneeze, the first word that comes from our mouth is, "we are dead la." That means we are dead dead, certainly dead, that is what Chinese people often say. They don't mean to curse themselves, but they get used to saying it and they don't realise their words have power.

Blessed and encouraging words are important. If we say things like "you will never come up with anything good, you always fail," then what happens to that person? He, or she will fail again, but if we change our words to positive, we bless them with positive words. Say things like "You are good and you will succeed. Sooner or later, eventually you will see the difference in their result.

Let us look at another example, the blessing of Isaac to Jacob. Isaac spoke the blessing through his words. All the words which he had spoken came to pass in Jacob's and his descendant's life.

So he went to him and kissed him. When Isaac caught the smell of his clothes, he blessed him and said, "Ah, the smell of my son is like the smell of a field that the Lord has blessed. May God give you heaven's dew and earth's richness— an abundance of grain and new wine. May nations serve you and peoples bow down to you. Be lord over your brothers, and may the sons of your mother bow down to you. May those who curse you be cursed and those who bless you be blessed." ***(Genesis 27:27-29)***

Be careful with your words, when we face difficulties, when we have good days or bad days, keep our attitude right, and speak positive words. Use your words to bless people not to curse. Believe that we have the favour of God. The words that come out from our mouths should reflect what we believe. If we believe we have the favour of God, we will speak the favour of God. Our speech must be full of positive words; we will surely see good days ahead.

THE FAVOUR OF GOD IS COMING OUR WAY. RECEIVE IT!

Chapter 10
Faith

Faith is an essential element of salvation. We need faith to continue our growth in the Lord. As previously discussed in the book, when we believe in Jesus and accept him as our Lord and saviour we already have the favour of God, but we need faith to activate it. As I said before, faith is to unlock the favour of God, as James said: *In the same way, faith by itself, if it is not accompanied by action, is dead* (James 2:17). Faith requires action.

In Mark's gospel it said: "have faith in God," that means to trust God, trust His word. When we trust His word, the favour of God will be released to us in a supernatural way. The blessing will be so vast it will overtake you. Believe that God will give you favour. In fact He is longing to give us favour and ask us to wait for His favour. As in the book of Isaiah:

Yet the Lord longs to be gracious to you; therefore he will rise up to show you compassion. For the Lord is a God of justice. Blessed are all who wait for him! ***(Isaiah 30:18)***

"Have faith in God," Jesus answered. "Truly I tell you, if anyone says to this mountain, 'Go, throw yourself into the sea,' and does not doubt in their heart but believes that what they say will happen, it will be done for them. Therefore I tell you, whatever you ask for in prayer, believe that you have received it, and it will be yours. ***(Mark 11:22-24)***

That was what Jesus said to His disciples, have faith in God, believe it and you will receive it.

We have to believe the word of God is important in order to activate the favour of God in our lives. John gospel says:

For God so loved the world that he gave his one and only Son, that whoever believes in him shall not perish but have eternal life. ***(John 3:16)***

If we believe it, we can have eternal life, if we don't believe it, we can't have eternal life. But we need faith to activate this verse, if we don't activate it with faith, it won't beneficial to our lives. The verse does not mean that all people will be saved, but only those who exercise their faith. Believe what His word says, and embrace it, those who do are saved.

The same is true, God's favour is following us, we have the favour of God in Christ, we need to activate it by faith, then God's favour is following us.

Don't be discouraged by your situation or circumstance, you just need to believe. Our God is a good God; He is longing to pour out His favour into our lives.

When you are in a difficult situation, you still need to believe the word of God. What He says He will do, He will do it.

EXAMPLE OF ABRAHAM:

Yet he did not waver through unbelief regarding the promise of God, but was strengthened in his faith and gave glory to God, 21 being fully persuaded that God had power to do what he had promised. ***(Romans 4:20-21)***

BY FAITH, DO SOMETHING THAT YOU HAVE NEVER DONE BEFORE, STEP OUT IN FAITH, YOU HAVE FAVOUR OF GOD IN YOUR LIFE. LET THE FIRE OF GOD BURN INSIDE YOUR HEART.

Chapter 11
Ask

Well, you may ask, if we believe Jesus then we already have the favour of God in our life. Why then do we need to ask for it? God can pour out his favour into our life at anytime, after all, He is sovereign God. Yes, it is true that God is absolute sovereign, but we can learn from some characters in the Bible who asked for God's favour. In the New Testament, Paul asked people to pray for the favour of God.

We do not want you to be uninformed, brothers and sisters, about the troubles we experienced in the province of Asia. We were under great pressure, far beyond our ability to endure, so that we despaired of life itself. Indeed, we felt we had received the sentence of death. But this happened that we might not rely on ourselves but on God, who raises the dead. He has delivered us from such a deadly peril, and he will deliver us again. On him we have set our hope that he will continue to deliver us, as you help us by your prayers. Then many will give thanks on our behalf for the gracious favor granted us in answer to the prayers of many. **(2 Corinthians 1:8-11)**

People prayed for the favour of God to be granted to Paul. In the Old Testament, Nehemiah also prayed for the favour of God.

Remember me with favor, my God, for all I have done for these people. **(Nehemiah 5:19)**

The favour of God was prayed for both in the Old and New Testaments. Even though we know it is God's will to pour out His favour into our lives, we still need to come into His presence and ask for it. Let us see another example from Daniel; he understood that the people of Israel had been in captivity for 70 years. It was God's will to set them free after 70 years, but he still prayed for their freedom. *in the first year of his reign, I, Daniel, understood from the Scriptures, according to the word of the Lord given to Jeremiah the prophet, that the desolation of Jerusalem would last seventy years. So I turned to the Lord God and pleaded with him in prayer and petition, in fasting, and in sackcloth and ashes. I prayed to the Lord my God and confessed: "Lord, the great and awesome God, who keeps his covenant of love with those who love him and keep his commandments,* **(Daniel 9:2-4)**

Even though Daniel knew that Israel would eventually be freed after 70 years in captivity, he still prayed about the matter. Why? I think the answer is, when he prayed, he knew it was God's will. If it is God's will, God would answer the prayer.

When we pray in accordance with the will of God (1 John 5:14) *This is the confidence we have in approaching God: that if we ask anything according to his will, he hears us.*

It gives us more confidence that it is God's will, so when we pray, we can have faith in that matter. We know we have favour, we know it is God who will give us favour when we pray. If we don't ask, we won't receive, as the book of James 4:2: *You do not have, because you do not ask God.*

I pray for myself, my family and the church. I ask God to give us favour and declare His favour upon our lives. The more you practice what you learn, pray, declare it, give thanks and exalt Jesus in every area of life. Your life will experience the supernatural favour of God. It gradually become very natural, God's favour will be upon your life, and His face will shine upon you.

EXAMPLE OF MOSES

He asked for God's favour.

Moses said to the Lord, "You have been telling me, 'Lead these people,' but you have not let me know whom you will send with me. You have said, 'I know you by name and you have found favor with me.' If you are pleased with me, teach me your ways so I may know you and continue to find favor with you. Remember that this nation is your people." **(Exodus 33:12-13)**

The more favour you ask for, the more favour you will receive. Our God loves to favour you.

Chapter 12
Give thanks

Realise that you have the favour of God and give thanks to Him always. Paul always gave thanks to God, in almost all of his letters.

*Rejoice always, pray continually, give thanks in all circumstances; for this is God's will for you in Christ Jesus. (**1 Thessalonians 5:16-18**)*

No matter what circumstance we are in, we should always give thanks to God. The secret is that when we give thanks to God, our attitude is different with the world's. Since the fall of mankind, people would not give thanks to God naturally because they blame God all the time. We as believers must give thanks to God, no matter what happens in our lives. When we give thanks to Him first, that means we acknowledge His presence and goodness. We acknowledge that He is the one who controls everything. Our heart is full of gratitude, even our prayers have not yet been answered, we choose to give thanks to Him first, When we do this, we invite God to show up in marvellous ways. You will see the favour of God coming.

Let me give you some examples: In Matthew chapter 14, the multitude followed Jesus and they did not have anything to eat, they only had two fishes and five loaves, before anything happened, before miracles appeared before their eyes, Jesus held the bread in His hands and He gave thanks to God. Suddenly miracles happened, the favour of God happened, the five loaves and two fishes fed five thousand men including women and children, probably twenty thousand people. They all ate and had more than enough, they had more than they needed.

Jesus gave thanks to God first before the miracle happened.

Another example is Mary's brother Lazarus, he was dead for four days. Jesus was sad but He came after four days. He first gave thanks to God. The favour of God appeared and a miracle took place, Lazarus came back to life. So they took away the stone. Then Jesus looked up and said,

"Father, I thank you that you have heard me. **(John 11:41)**

When he had said this, Jesus called in a loud voice, "Lazarus, come out!" **(John 11:43)**

The ten lepers got healed in Luke 17:11-19, but only one came back to Jesus and thanked Him. Only the one who came back and thanked Jesus got complete healing, physical and spiritual healing.

When Paul and Silas were in jail, they praised God first. After they praised God a miracle took place, the earth shook and the favour of God came.

About midnight Paul and Silas were praying and singing hymns to God, and the other prisoners were listening to them. Suddenly there was such a violent earthquake that the foundations of the prison were shaken. At once all the prison doors flew open, and everyone's chains came loose. **(Acts 16:25-26)**

When you give thanks to God, the favour of God will come to you, even in a prison cell, like Joseph or Paul and Silas. Even when there seems to be no way out, give thanks to God first and praise Him.

Put Jesus at the centre of our lives. Always thank Him first; no matter what situation you are in. Even if you have no job, no money, or your relationships are broken; always remember to give thanks to him.

We need to understand the law of heaven, which operates differently to earth. Worldly people only give thanks to God when they receive something, we should give thanks at all times. Even if you have no job, you should give thanks to Him first, this is how the law of heaven works, the Bible says in Luke 6:38, give, and it will be given to you. You give first and then receive.

If we give thanks to God in every circumstance, no matter what happens in our life, the enemy will become very scared of you. Giving thanks to God first is a powerful weapon that we can use to destroy our enemies. It can change the spiritual atmosphere.

When we look in the Bible at people who received the favour of God, many of those people were in difficult situations. Despite this they still gave thanks to God, people like Paul experienced real hardship, difficulty, imprisoned, was beaten, stoned and flogged thirty nine times, yet he still gave thanks to God first.

When we are in difficult times, it is the right time to show our faith and give thanks to God. Most of us have no problem thanking God when times are good. The real test comes when times are not so good.

King David was definitely a person so blessed and favoured by God. In spite of everything he went through he always remembered to thank and praise God. As we can see in many of the psalms that he wrote, thanksgiving filled up his heart and his life no matter what the situation.

Give thanks to the LORD, for he is good; his love endures forever. **(Psalm 118:1)**

Open for me the gates of the righteous; I will enter and give thanks to the LORD. **(Psalm 118:19)**

I will give you thanks, for you answered me; you have become my salvation. **(Psalm 118:21)**

Even in face of enemies he praised and gave thanks to God. In times of being oppressed, his thanksgiving attracted God's favour.

**GET EXCITED ABOUT GOD'S FAVOUR.
IT IS COMING TO YOU NOW. THANK HIM FOR HIS FAVOUR.**

Chapter 13
Exalt Jesus

Remember to always exalt Jesus whether in the good times or bad times.

Therefore God exalted him to the highest place and gave him the name that is above every name, ***(Philippians 2:9)***

Father God exalted Jesus to a higher place, God wants Jesus to manifest His power. God wants everyone to acknowledge His Son Jesus. If we exalt Jesus in everything, it will please God the Father as it is God's will that Jesus be lifted up and for all people to acknowledge Him.

And a voice from heaven said, "This is my Son, whom I love; with him I am well pleased." ***(Matthew 3:17)***

While he was still speaking, a bright cloud covered them, and a voice from the cloud said, "This is my

Son, whom I love; with him I am well pleased. Listen to him!" **(Matthew 17:5)**

He will glorify me because it is from me that he will receive what he will make known to you. **(John 16:14)**

The Holy Spirit loves Jesus, loves to glorify Jesus, He loves to talk about Jesus, He loves to exalt Jesus.

The Father God loves Jesus, and God always exalted Jesus. In our everyday life, we should exalt Jesus in every area of our lives. We must acknowledge His presence. When we are in our work place, we should exalt Jesus, wherever we go, we should exalt Jesus. We should let people know Christ lives in us, and dare to represent Jesus to people. You will see the favour of God overtake you.

John the Baptist always exalted Jesus, when he saw Jesus coming to him, he pointed people to Jesus, he exalted Jesus and he said:

The next day John saw Jesus coming toward him and said, "Look, the Lamb of God, who takes away the sin of the world! This is the one I meant when I said, 'A man who comes after me has surpassed me because he was before me.' **(John 1:29-30)**

You yourselves can testify that I said, 'I am not the Messiah but am sent ahead of him.' **(John 3:28)**

He must become greater, I must become less. **(John 3:30)**

EXAMPLE OF PAUL

When we look at Pauls' letters we read: For *I resolved to know nothing while I was with you except Jesus Christ and him crucified.* **(1 Corinthians 2:2)**

I eagerly expect and hope that I will in no way be ashamed, but will have sufficient courage so that now as always Christ will be exalted in my body, whether by life or by death. **(Philippians 1:20)**

I have been crucified with Christ and I no longer live, but Christ lives in me. The life I now live in the body, I live by faith in the Son of God, who loved me and gave himself for me. **(Galatians 2:20)**

Paul received much favour from God.

I thank Christ Jesus our Lord, who has given me strength, that he considered me trustworthy, appointing me to his service. Even though I was once a blasphemer and a persecutor and a violent man, I was shown mercy because I acted in ignorance and unbelief. The grace of our Lord was poured out on me abundantly, along with the faith and love that are in Christ Jesus. **(1 Timothy 1:12-14)**

No matter what situation we are in, we must dare to exalt His name in every circumstance and acknowledge Him.

"Whoever acknowledges me before others, I will also acknowledge before my Father in heaven. But whoever disowns me before others, I will disown before my Father in heaven. **(Matthew 10:32-33)**

When we acknowledge His presence, exalt His name in all situations, even when we are in difficulty, God will turn our negative situation around into a positive outcome because you exalt His name. The favour of God will come to you when you exalt His name.

HIS FAVOUR IS LIKE A RIVER FLOODING INTO YOUR LIFE

Chapter 14
Declare the words

The final key is to declare His word. Declare that you have the favour of God, make a declaration in the heavenly realm. It is very important and we should speak it loud. Surely goodness and love will follow you all the days of your life, your cup overflows.

Declare that all the good things will follow you, your family will prosper, your business will be successful, your relationships will be positive, just declare all the good things that you want to happen. It is important to make a declaration.

Why do we need to make a declaration? When YOU make a declaration in heaven, the spiritual realm is shifting according to what YOU declare. The spiritual atmosphere will be changed; all heavenly beings know and hear what YOU declare. Because you directly proclaim it in heaven, satan will be scared and shaken.

When you declare it openly, speak it loudly so that your inner man can hear it and your faith will be increased.

Below are only a few examples of verses we can use to make a declaration over our lives.

The LORD will make you the head not the tail..... You will always be at the top, never at the bottom. **(Deuteronomy 28:13)**

Surely, Lord, you bless the righteous; you surround them with your favor as with a shield. **(Psalm 5:12)**

You prepare a table before me in the presence of my enemies. You anoint my head with oil; my cup overflows. Surely your goodness and love will follow me all the days of my life, and I will dwell in the house of the Lord forever. **(Psalm 23:5-6)**

For his anger lasts only a moment, but his favor lasts a lifetime; weeping may stay for the night, but rejoicing comes in the morning. **(Psalm 30:5)**

Then you will win favor and a good name in the sight of God and man. **(Proverbs 3:4)**

Very truly I tell you, whoever believes in me will do the works I have been doing, and they will do even *greater things than these, because I am going to the Father.***(John 14:12)**

I can do all this through him who gives me strength. **(Philippians 4:13)**

Don't be discouraged by other people, declare it by faith. Declare it every day. Say that the goodness, love and favour of God will follow. You will see your life and your family will be different. Good things from God will come to you in a supernatural way.

I declare it every day for myself, for my family and for my church. I usually say, "In the name of Jesus, goodness, love and mercy will follow me, the favour of God will follow me. I am healthy. I am successful. I am the head and not the tail. I am the top and not the bottom."

Declarations are powerful, the Bible says you shall also decree a thing and it shall be established to you.

*Thou shalt also decree a thing, and it shall be established unto thee: and the light shall shine upon thy ways .***(Job 22:28)**

I still remember when I first preached about this subject the favour of God. I encouraged my church members to declare that we have favour of God. An amazing thing happened, many people gave their testimonies about how God favoured them. Some people testified about how God gave them parking space when they drove to Chinatown in central London. We all know parking in Chinatown is very difficult especially on a Sunday afternoon. But every time they pray for God's favour when they drove to Chinatown, amazingly, they always found a good space to park their car.

YOU CAN MAKE THE FOLLOWING DECLARATION: IN THE NAME OF JESUS:

1. I am the head not the tail
2. I am excellent
3. I am rich
4. I am healthy
5. I am highly favoured and greatly blessed
6. I am powerful
7. I am a child of God
8. I am intelligent
9. I am fruitful
10. I am successful

11. I have the wisdom of God
12. I can do all things through Christ
13. I soar on wings like eagles
14. I love God with all heart.

<u>EXAMPLE OF JESUS</u>

Jesus was so highly favoured because He is the Son of the most high. In all circumstances, He declares God's goodness and grace. He fully understood how the spiritual realm operates. He always declares positively, even in hopeless situations, which draws the full measure of favour from the heaven.

JESUS DECLARES HIS IDENTITY.

Then Jesus declared, "I, the one speaking to you—I am he." **(John 4:26)**

Then Jesus declared, "I am the bread of life. Whoever comes to me will never go hungry, and whoever believes in me will never be thirsty. **(John 6:35)**

Meanwhile, all the people were wailing and mourning for her. "Stop wailing," Jesus said. "She is not dead but asleep." **(Luke 8:52)**

After he had said this, he went on to tell them, "Our friend Lazarus has fallen asleep; but I am going there to wake him up." His disciples replied, "Lord, if he sleeps, he will get better." Jesus had been speaking of his death, but his disciples thought he meant natural sleep. **(John 11:11-13)**

Jesus declares that Jairus' daughter and Lazarus were asleep, not dead. In the hopeless situation, Jairus' daughter and Lazarus were dead, Lazarus was dead for four days, but Jesus said he had fallen asleep. Jesus called out in a loud voice, Lazarus came out. (John 11:43) The dead man came out alive. We can see how powerful the word of Jesus is.

DECLARE THAT YOU HAVE THE FAVOUR OF GOD.

Chapter 15
Receive God's Favour

RECEIVE GOD'S FAVOUR

God has already ordained us to receive His favour, grace and blessings. He has not just randomly given it to us, He destined us to receive grace before time began.

No, we declare God's wisdom, a mystery that has been hidden and that God destined for our glory before time began. **(1 Corinthians 2:7)**

When we talk about the favour of God, God not only want to give us material blessings. I find the most important and valuable blessing is in the spiritual realm. When God favours us, He opens the eyes of our heart. He helps us to see the things that we are unable to see with our human eyes. He gives us revelation.

Let me give you some examples:

God revealed to Abraham the things to come, He gave him revelation. Abraham was a friend of God, because God talked to him face to face. This is the favour of God. We should not only desire material things, but we must also desire to be closer to God. We must want to hear His voice, and want Him to give us spiritual revelation.

Then the Lord said, "Shall I hide from Abraham what I am about to do? **(Genesis 18:17)**

God revealed to Abraham his future and also revealed to him that He was about to destroy the city.

Another person we need to mention is Mary.

Then Mary took about a pint[a] of pure nard, an expensive perfume; she poured it on Jesus' feet and wiped his feet with her hair. And the house was filled with the fragrance of the perfume. **(John 12:3)**

"Leave her alone," Jesus replied. "It was intended that she should save this perfume for the day of my burial. You will always have the poor among you, but you will not always have me." **(John 12:7-8)**

Mary poured her perfume, worth a year's wages onto the feet of Jesus. Many viewed her actions as a waste. She saw the one thing that others did not see; she had the revelation that others did not have. She knew that Jesus would not be with them on earth much longer. She needed to take the opportunity she had to serve Jesus; otherwise she would never have the opportunity to serve Him again. She took this time to do what was right.

Other people did not see that. Why? Because that specific revelation was given to her. The Lord showed favour to her by revealing those things and giving insight.

How about the two disciples walking with Jesus they didn't even know who accompanied with. (Luke 24:13-49) They did not know it was Jesus, until Jesus opened the eyes of their heart, so that they realised it was Jesus. They received the favour of God.

Apostle John received the favour of God and saw the risen Lord in glory and Jesus revealed to him the things of the future, Jesus gave him the revelation (Revelation 1), this was also the favour of God.

We want God to give us revelation when we read His word, and when we minister to people. We want Jesus to manifest in us so people will truly see the favour of God is in our lives.

MY PERSONAL ENCOUNTER WITH GOD.

When I look back on my life, I have received much favour from God. Without His favour in my life, it would be impossible to have become what I am now.

I experience His favour in my life every day, sometimes He grants me the desires of my heart before I even ask Him.

On another occasion, I was thinking I would like to eat some noodles. I ended up ordering something a little cheaper, but in my heart, I really wanted to eat noodles. Surprisingly, the manager of the restaurant brought a dish of noodles to me and said, because the next table made a mistake in their order, this noodle dish is for you, free of charge. The favour of God comes even before we ask. God fulfils our hearts desires; He knows every part of our lives, even our inmost being.

You know when I sit and when I rise; you perceive my thoughts from afar. You discern my going out and my lying down; you are familiar with all my ways. Before a word is on my tongue you, Lord, know it completely. **(Psalm 139:2-4)**

Throughout this book we have explored the many people God chose to favour in the Bible.

Noah:

This is the account of Noah and his family. Noah was a righteous man, blameless among the people of his time, and he walked faithfully with God. **(Genesis 6:9)**

Abraham:

But Abram said to the king of Sodom, "With raised hand I have sworn an oath to the Lord, God Most High, Creator of heaven and earth, that I will accept nothing belonging to you, not even a thread or the strap of a sandal, so that you will never be able to say, 'I made Abram rich.' **(Genesis 14:22-23)**

Joseph:

*No one is greater in this house than I am. My master has withheld nothing from me except you, because you are his wife. How then could I do such a wicked thing and sin against God?"***(Genesis 39:9)**

Esther:

"Go, gather together all the Jews who are in Susa, and fast for me. Do not eat or drink for three days, night or day. I and my attendants will fast as you do. When this is done, I will go to the king, even though it is against the law. And if I perish, I perish." **(Esther 4:16)**

Mary:

"I am the Lord's servant," Mary answered. "May your word to me be fulfilled." Then the angel left her. **(Luke 1:38)** *She was highly favour by God.*

Paul:

However, I consider my life worth nothing to me; my only aim is to finish the race and complete the task the Lord Jesus has given me—the task of testifying to the good news of God's grace. **(Acts 20:24)**

All of these people have one thing in common; they all took God very seriously. They were God fearing people and were willing to do whatever it took to remain in right standing with God. They committed to living their lives for God and so the favour of God followed them. God is love, He always wants to give us the best. He always wants to pour out His grace upon our lives.

We need to receive His favour and believe what He says in His WORD. We should trust His WORD, be a doer of His WORD. Position yourself to receive the favour of God.

HE LOVES YOU.

Chapter 16
Testimonies of God's favour

I just wanted to let you know that the book you were writing has so much power and favour in it. I received so much favour from God since I was translating the book so I just want to share some testimonies with you.

I went back to China two weeks ago and my flight landed in Hong Kong so I needed to cross the border to go to Shenzhen. When I got off the car with my parents, I saw the queue in the custom border is extremely long and I was thinking I have to wait for a long time, but a middle-age guy worked from the Custom just found me and asked are you Esther? And he pulled me over to the front of the queue and I skipped the whole queue and passed the border with my parents.

I thought it was my dad's friend because he used to work at the border but neither of my parents knows him but He knows me so he helped us skip the whole line. Few days later, I also experienced the same thing coming back from Hong Kong, when I was queuing, a new window at the border was opened for me so that I become the first person again to pass. During the two weeks break, I went to some restaurants, people are waiting outside but whenever I went, I don't need to wait and the waitress can always find seats for me and my friends. I know that's God's favour.

The other thing is that I bought a keyboard when I was in Philadelphia I wasn't able to bring it with me to Redding, I was hoping to sell it last year but no one is buying it, so I kept it at my friend's house, but two day ago my friend told me there were a few people want to buy my keyboard and one by one they are giving a higher price and yesterday my friend sold it to the person who gave the highest price. I know it's God favour and he really blessed me with that because I almost forgot I had that keyboard and I need to sell it. But God remembered it and he brought buyers to buy my keyboard.

The last thing is that I booked the round trip ticket from London to Bethel last summer and I found out my return ticket is on May 9th but my graduation is on the 16th, when I checked online I need to pay almost 200-300 pounds to make the date changes, so I decided to pray and call the airline company and see whether it makes a difference. At the end of the conversation, the customer service person changed my flight after my graduation date and he also changed my flight from a connecting flight to a direct flight so that I don't need to transfer (I used to have transfer from Los Angeles to London) without paying any money! All the changes are FREE! I know this is the favour from God again!

I wrote this to you and just want to thank you to let me join in the process translating this and I am experiencing so much God's favour while translating and even now. I know this book would surely bless so many people and your anointing and power will flow through the book and whoever reads it would also experience God's favour!

Favour after reading the hand writing version of this book. (Esther)

'I graduated 2 years ago from the university that I favoured, and since then I have been in search for job opportunities and greater experiences in the design industry. However, at the time, it was a very difficult situation, and as a freelancer, my income was very unstable and financially needing a breakthrough.

I still remembered quite clearly, after praying and deciding to trust God for His provision to stay and work in London, shortly after that I was offered a paid internship placement in a global design company for 3 months. And as the end of my placement approached, my contract was extended, however it was with no promise of a full time job offer since the company had other plans in mind.

But through God's favour, a door was opened for me on the very last day, as the founder of the company changed his mind all of a sudden and opened a brand new position for me as a junior designer with a competitive salary. It was a miracle to me, that God has made the impossible possible by His power. And since then He has opened my mind to expect and receive even more of His abundance favour in every detail of my life.

Favour in job. (Q. Wong)

I started teaching in my current school three years ago. When I first started, I only had one year experience of teaching however when I had my interview, the head teacher was very impressed. It is normal to go up one pay scale each year of teaching, but I went up 3 years only in the first year. God is really good. It is God's favour.

In my second year of teaching, an opportunity for promotion from Maths teacher to Head of A-Level Maths came up so I decided to apply even though I had only been in the school for one year and in teaching for two years. In this promotion, I had a lot of favour from God from the interviewer and heads of School and had another pay rise along with it.

My experience of teaching is little compared to many teachers in the school who have been there 10, 20 years however my salary is similar to those who have at least 6 years teaching experience. God has really used me in this school not only to bless my career but also to make a difference in the children.

I am now only in my third year of teaching at this school, and After having been Head of A-levels for 6 months, God opened up another opportunity for promotion to second in Charge of Maths department.

Normally, those in this position are twice my age with many more years of teaching experience. Before attending the interview, I had been standing in as Acting Head of Maths department because the usual teacher had injured herself which meant that I was fully equipped and trained for the position for Second in Charge. Praise God that I got the promotion! Really give thanks to God for His plans to bless me and equip me with the skills and knowledge to be the best.

It was God's favour on my life again. I received favour upon favour in my life.

Favour in career (Li)

INVITATION TO SALVATION

If you want to become a Christian believer and follow Jesus right now you can pray this prayer below:

Heavenly Father!

I come to you in prayer, confessing all my sins. I believe Jesus died on the cross for my sins and I want to accept Jesus Christ as my Lord and personal saviour.

I repent and ask that you will forgive me of all of my sins. Today I make a choice to follow you.

Please come into my heart and pour out your favour into my life. In Jesus name I pray.

Amen.

But what does it say? "The word is near you; it is in your mouth and in your heart," that is, the message concerning faith that we proclaim. If you declare with your mouth, "Jesus is Lord," and believe in your heart that God raised him from the dead, you will be saved. For it is with your heart that you believe and are justified, and it is with your mouth that you profess your faith and are saved. Scripture says, "Anyone who believes in him will never be put to shame. For there is no difference between Jew and Gentile—the same Lord is Lord of all and richly blesses all who call on him, for, everyone who calls on the name of the Lord will be saved. "How, then, can they call on the one they have not believed in? And how can they believe in the one of whom they have not heard? And how can they hear without someone preaching to them? And how can anyone preach unless they are sent? As it is written: "How beautiful are the feet of those who bring good news!" But not all the Israelites accepted the good news. For Isaiah says, "Lord, who has believed our message?" Consequently, faith comes from hearing the message, and the message is heard through the word about Christ. **(Romans 10:8-17)**

God bless you.

Rev. Dr. Bobby Sung

www.sungministry.com

Favour of God Notes

Favour of God Notes

....

....

....

....

....

....

....

....

....

....

....

....

....

....

....

....

....

....

....

....

....

....

....

....

Favour of God Notes

Favour of God Notes

Favour of God Notes

Favour of God Notes

ALSO WRITTEN BY DR. SUNG

PAPERBACKS AVAILABLE AT SUNGMINISTRY.COM
AND ALL GOOD BOOKSTORES

EBOOK VERSIONS ALSO AVAILABLE ON APPLE®
AMAZON KINDLE

Lightning Source UK Ltd.
Milton Keynes UK
UKOW02f0151100316

269912UK00001B/14/P